D0621057

BOSTON UNIVERSITY STUDIES IN
PHILOSOPHY AND RELIGION
General Editor: Leroy S. Rouner
Volume Thirteen

Selves, People, and Persons:

What Does It Mean to Be a Self?

Edited by

Leroy S. Rouner

UNIVERSITY OF NOTRE DAME PRESS

Notre Dame, Indiana

Copyright © 1992
University of Notre Dame Press
Notre Dame, Indiana 46556
All Rights Reserved

Library of Congress Cataloging-in-Publication Data

Selves, people, and persons : what does it mean to be a
self? / Leroy S. Rouner, editor.
    p.   cm. — (Boston University studies in phi-
losophy and religion ; v. 13)
  Includes index.
  ISBN 0-268-01747-6
  1. Self (Philosophy)   2. Philosophical anthro-
pology.   I. Rouner, Leroy S.   II. Series.
BD450.S3935   1992
126 — dc20   92-53748
                                                  CIP

Manufactured in the United States of America

For Ninian Smart

His Institute lectures have introduced us to a larger world of religious world views. Having overcome exclusiveness in his personal adaptation of Buddhist ideas to Christianity, he shows us a pacific world of creative religious variety grounded in our common humanity.

Contents

Preface

Boston University Studies in Philosophy and Religion is a joint project of the Boston University Institute for Philosophy and Religion and the University of Notre Dame Press. The essays in each annual volume are edited from the previous year's lecture program and invited papers of the Boston University Institute. The Director of the Institute, who is also the Editor of these Studies, chooses a theme and invites participants to lecture at Boston University in the course of the academic year. The Editor then selects and edits the essays to be included in the volume. In preparation is Volume 14, *Can Virtue Be Taught?*

The Boston University Institute for Philosophy and Religion was begun informally in 1970 under the leadership of Professor Peter Bertocci of the Department of Philosophy, with the cooperation of Dean Walter Muelder of the School of Theology, Professor James Purvis, Chair of the Department of Religion, and Professor Marx Wartofsky, Chair of the Department of Philosophy. Professor Bertocci was concerned to institutionalize one of the most creative features of Boston personalism, its interdisciplinary approach to fundamental issues of human life. When Professor Leroy S. Rouner became Director in 1975, and the Institute became a formal Center of the Boston University Graduate School, every effort was made to continue that vision of an ecumenical and interdisciplinary forum.

Within the University the Institute is committed to open interchange on fundamental issues in philosophy and religious study which transcend the narrow specializations of academic curricula. We seek to counter those trends in higher education which emphasize technical expertise in a "multi-versity," and gradually transform undergraduate liberal arts education into preprofessional training.

Our programs are open to the general public, and are regularly broadcast on WBUR-FM, Boston University's National Public Radio affiliate. Outside the University we seek to recover the public tradition of philosophical discourse which was a lively part of American intellectual life in the early years of this century before the professionalization of both philosophy and religious reflection made these two disciplines topics virtually unavailable even to an educated public. We note, for example, that much of William James's work was presented originally as public lectures, and we are grateful to James's present-day successors for the significant public papers which we have been honored to publish. This commitment to a public tradition in American intellectual life has important stylistic implications. At a time when too much academic writing is incomprehensible, or irrelevant, or both, our goal is to present readable essays by acknowledged authorities on critical human issues.

Acknowledgments

Our authors have been generous in their commitment to our program, and gracious in response to my editing. The Institute is honored by their participation, and grateful to each of them.

Copy editing and manuscript preparation is a labor of love performed annually by Dr. Barbara Darling-Smith, Assistant to the Director of the Institute. She does this complex and occasionally exasperating task with high energy, good humor, and dazzling expertise. This year she has been assisted by Denice K. Carnes.

Ann Rice at the University of Notre Dame Press guides the manuscript through the publication process with professional poise, and a gift for making sure that the right thing gets done at the right time. Jim Langford, Director of the University of Notre Dame Press, has been a participant in our programs, and an invaluable colleague. His expert advice and enthusiasm for this series continues to be one of the Institute's major resources.

This year's program has been made possible by a generous grant from the Lilly Endowment, Inc. Our special thanks to Craig Dykstra and Jeanne Knoerle for their support.

Contributors

LAWRENCE E. CAHOONE received his Ph.D. in philosophy at the State University of New York at Stony Brook in 1985. The author of *The Dilemma of Modernity: Philosophy, Culture, and Anti-Culture* (published by the State University of New York Press in 1988), as well as many articles, he is completing *Inquiry without Limits.* He was the recipient of a Eugene M. Kayden National University Press Book Award in 1989 and is a member of the Advisory Board for *Thémata: Revista De Filosofía* at the Universidad de Sevilla. He is Assistant Professor of Philosophy at Boston University.

JOHN B. CARMAN is Parkman Professor of Divinity and Professor of Comparative Religion at Harvard Divinity School. He studied at Haverford College, Yale University, and the University of Leiden and has also lived and taught in India. He has written many articles and books on Hindu life and thought, relations between Christians and Hindus, and the comparative study of religion — among them *The Theology of Ramanuja* and *The Tamil Veda: Pillan's Interpretation of the Tiruvaymoli;* and his contribution to the Eerdmans series *Studies in a Christian World View,* entitled *Majesty and Mercy: Contrasts and Harmonies in the Concept of God,* is in preparation.

ELIOT DEUTSCH received his Ph.D. from Columbia University and is now Professor of Philosophy at the University of Hawaii. He succeeded Charles Moore, and served until recently as Editor of *Philosophy East and West*. He continues in an editorial capacity for a number of scholarly publications including the *Journal of Chinese Philosophy* and the *Journal of Buddhist Philosophy*. His books include *Personhood, Creativity, and Freedom* and *Interpreting Across Boundaries: New Essays in Comparative Philosophy* (edited with Gerald Larson).

EDWARD W. JAMES is Professor of Philosophy at Bridgewater (Massachusetts) State College, and he has also taught at Bates College. His Ph.D. is in philosophy from the University of Southern California, and he received his A.B. from Tufts University. The recipient of an NDEA Fellowship, Professor James has published essays in *Mind, Ethics, Philosophy*, and *The Journal of Speculative Philosophy*, as well as in an earlier volume of BOSTON UNIVERSITY STUDIES IN PHILOSOPHY AND RELIGION, *Foundations of Ethics: The Right and the Good*.

ERAZIM KOHÁK is Professor of Philosophy at Boston University and at Univerzita Karlova in Prague. He grew up in Czechoslovakia, was exiled in 1948, and emigrated to the United States in 1949. He studied at Colgate University and Yale Divinity School and received his Ph.D. from Yale University Graduate School. Professor Kohák is the author of several books, including *Idea and Experience: Edmund Husserl's Project of Phenomenology in Ideas I* and *The Embers and the Stars: A Philosophical Inquiry into the Moral Sense of Nature*. His 1972 book *The Victors and the Vanquished* (with H. Kovály) was named the *New York Times Book Review* book of the year in 1973.

LIVIA KOHN is Assistant Professor of Religion at Boston University. She has also taught at the Universität Göttingen and in the Department of Asian Languages and Cultures at the University of Michigan. She is editor of *Taoist Meditation and*

Longevity Techniques and author of two books currently in press: *Early Chinese Mysticism: Philosophy and Soteriology in the Taoist Tradition* and *Taoist Mystical Philosophy: The Scripture of Western Ascension.* She is also managing editor of *Taoist Resources.* She was born and grew up in West Germany and received her Ph.D. at Bonn University.

JOHN E. MACK is Professor of Psychiatry at Harvard Medical School at Cambridge Hospital, where he teaches psychiatric residents and trainees. He did his residency training at Massachusetts Mental Health Center and is a graduate of the Boston Psychoanalytic Institute in child and adult psychoanalysis. He is also Founding Director of the Center for Psychological Studies in the Nuclear Age. His writings cover a wide range of topics: from adolescent suicide and nightmares in human conflict to a biography of a woman Holocaust survivor. He won a Pulitzer Prize in biography for his book *A Prince of our Disorder: The Life of T. E. Lawrence.*

HAROLD H. OLIVER is Professor of Philosophical Theology at Boston University, and he has also taught at Rice University, Southeastern Baptist Theological Seminary, and Emory University. He received his A.B. from Samford University, his B.D. from Southern Baptist Theological Seminary, his Th.M. from Princeton Theological Seminary, and his Ph.D. from Emory University, where he has also done postdoctoral study. Last year he was president of the Karl Jaspers Society of North America. He is the author of numerous articles and has translated a number of Fritz Buri's works. Professor Oliver's own books include *Relatedness: Essays in Metaphysics and Theology* and *A Relational Metaphysic: Studies in Philosophy and Religion 4.*

BHIKHU PAREKH grew up in India and received his B.A. and M.A. at Ruia College, Bombay, and the Bombay School of Economics. He received his Ph.D. from the London School of Economics. He has taught political theory at Hull University since 1964. In 1981 he returned to India and was Vice-Chancellor (President) of Baroda University until 1984. In Britain he served from 1985 to 1990 as Deputy Chairman of the Commission for Racial Equality. His many books include *Hannah Arendt and the Search for a New Political Philosophy; Karl Marx's Theory of Ideology; Contemporary Political Thinkers; Gandhi's Political Philosophy;* and *Colonialism, Tradition, and Reform: An Analysis of Gandhi's Political Discourse.*

LEROY S. ROUNER is Professor of Philosophy, Religion and Philosophical Theology; and Director of the Institute for Philosophy and Religion at Boston University. He is General Editor of Boston University Studies in Philosophy and Religion and has also edited *Philosophy, Religion, and the Coming World Civilization, The Wisdom of Ernest Hocking* (with John Howie) and *Corporations and the Common Good* (with Robert Dickie). He is the author of *Within Human Experience, The Long Way Home* (a memoir), and, most recently, *To Be At Home: Christianity, Civil Religion and World Community.*

KRISTER STENDAHL is now the Myra and Robert Kraft and Jacob Hiatt Distinguished Professor of Christian Studies at Brandeis University. Born and raised in Stockholm, Sweden, and educated at Uppsala University, he was ordained in 1944 and served as parish pastor. He spent thirty years at Harvard Divinity School, eleven of them as Dean, and left there as Andrew W. Mellon Professor of Divinity emeritus, to serve as Bishop of Stockholm in his native Church of Sweden. His special interests are Jewish-Christian relations and the role of women in the Bible, as reflected in his many books: *The School of St. Matthew, The Bible and the Role of Women, Holy Week, Paul among Jews and Gentiles, Meanings,* and *Energy for Life.*

ALFRED I. TAUBER received his B.S. and his M.D. from Tufts
University. He is Professor of Medicine and Professor of Pa-
thology at Boston University's School of Medicine and is also
Adjunct Professor of Biology at the College of Liberal Arts at
Boston University. He has been Clinical Fellow and Research
Fellow in Medicine (Hematology) at Tufts–New England
Medical Center as well as Research Fellow in Medicine at
Harvard Medical School and Robert B. Brigham Hospital
(Boston). The author of numerous articles in medical jour-
nals, Dr. Tauber has also written (with Leon Chernyak)
*Metchnikoff and the Origins of Immunology: From Meta-
phor to Theory* and has edited *Organism and the Origins
of Self.*

Introduction

LEROY S. ROUNER

"I am."

This, at least, we know for sure. Common sense accepts the affirmation intuitively. To think otherwise is probably impossible, and surely pathological. The certain knowledge of self-identity is crucial for our sanity. And philosophical traditions as diverse as the Hindu nondualism of Śankara, the Christian philosophy of Augustine, and the modernism of Descartes are agreed that the affirmation of selfhood is the axiom which gives philosophy its point of departure. Any thought presupposes a thinker who has the thought. Descartes's *cogito ergo sum* ("I think, therefore I am") is the most succinct expression of this point, but it is based on Augustine's *si fallor sum* ("If I err, I am") and has a precise equivalent in Śankara's commentary on the *Brahma Sutra*, where he argues that "all means of knowledge exist only as dependent on self-experience and since such experience is its own proof there is no necessity for proving the existence of the self."[1]

But the meaning of selfhood has become an urgent question, largely in reaction to the radical individualism in which many modern Western notions of selfhood have been cast. That rugged individualism which was so long celebrated as the quintessentially American life of high energy and imaginative creativity has been challenged by a new communitarianism. In the philosophy of Alasdair MacIntyre's *After Virtue* and Huston Smith's *Beyond the PostModern Mind*, the sociology of Robert Bellah's *Habits of the Heart*, the ecology of Thomas Berry's *Dream of the Earth*, the feminism of Rosemary Ruether's *New Woman, New Earth*, and the economics of E. F. Schumacher's *Small is Beautiful*, individualism is challenged and the new communitarianism celebrated. In cross-cultural dialogue, Buddhist philosophers like David Kalupa-

1

hana of Sri Lanka and Masao Abe of the Kyoto School in Japan now make common cause with the American pragmatist William James, using the doctrine of "pure experience" as the metaphysical basis for the paradoxical notion of the "no-self." This "selfless" notion of the self criticizes the individualistic, rights-oriented understanding of selfhood as leading to the self-centeredness of the "me" generation, the ecological destructiveness of the consumer society, and the political exploitation of Third World countries and their natural resources.

Among our authors, only Harry Oliver proposes a "no-self" doctrine, but numerous others agree with him that selves are always to be understood in relation to the communities of which they are a part. Even if some sense of individual selfhood seems inescapable, most of our authors qualify the free-standing and largely self-determining picture of the individual self which was associated with American heroes from the lonely settler and pioneer to the modern entrepreneur. In so doing they are reshaping fundamental ideas of the self in fields as various as theology, biology, psychoanalysis, and political philosophy.

Our first group of essays deals with ground issues in the philosophy of selfhood. We begin with Erazim Kohák's title essay on "Selves, People, Persons: An Essay in American Personalism." A Czech scholar who has done extensive work on Husserl's phenomenology, Kohák identifies with the Boston personalism which once dominated the department where he now teaches. For personalism, as for existentialism, being a person did not mean belonging to the species *homo sapiens sapiens*. A person is rather a task to which we are called. More than that, it was not just a mode of being human, but a fundamental metaphysical category in which reality is defined as a community of persons. Within that community humans have a special task and a special responsibility which defines the distinctively human way of being a person. To be a person, then, is first of all to have the disparate moments of one's experience unified by a role or agenda, along with a distinctive style in going about fulfilling that agenda. We live in a value-laden, meaningfully ordered world, so a person is a being who can grieve, cherish, respect, and care in a world of good and evil. And such a person fulfills life's agenda not arbitrarily but appropriately, in regard to those rules which demand respectful demeanor toward oneself and others.

Kohák notes that personalism's social program was so prominent and appealing that its metaphysical foundations became lost. Much of his essay is given to a reconstruction of this metaphysics, arguing that subject is an irreducible category in the economy of the cosmos. The world is a meaningful ordering, in which all relations are essentially the subject relations of *near* and *dear*. "Nearness" is not an extensional relation, but a meaningful relation of value, or "dearness." Treating the world as object is legitimate and useful for certain purposes, but it is not metaphysically fundamental. This is not to say, however, that we live in a subjective world, like that of Fichte's idealism. The personalists did not argue that thought gives rise to matter, except in the primordial case of God's creation of the world. Kohák likens Boston personalism to the transcendental idealism of Husserl. There is a problem, however, in treating all levels of reality as persons. That problem is the paralysis of universal compassion. What is needed is a hierarchy of value, and that is difficult to articulate. Specifically, what is the distinctiveness of the human person? What justifies our instinctive placing of ourselves as normative in the cosmic hierarchy? Kohák argues that we are the species without a natural habitat. We have moved from a natural to a cultural environment and therefore must justify ourselves in a way that other species need not do. He concludes that we are the species that can bring eternity into time. "Humans can know the true, honor the good, cherish the beautiful." And when we fail to do that, the world is better left to those species with a natural habitat, like the coyotes.

Harold Oliver's essay on "The Relational Self" shares many of Kohák's personalistic concerns, particularly the notion that reality is a community of beings. He differs, however, in his understanding of selfhood. Kohák sees the person as the ultimate reality; Oliver sees reality not in terms of substantive selves, but in terms of the relations which the self has with others. Hence, for him, what is real is not the self *per se*, but the event in which the self — in Kohák's terms — acts purposively on its agenda. In that act the self is in relation to some other. Oliver's argument is that to be a self is always to be in this act of relation, and that selfhood is therefore defined by this act of relating. The true self is always the self-in-relation. Therefore Oliver argues that the relation is what is real, and that the "self" which becomes real in this act of relating is real only in the relation.

This view goes against the intuitions of most Western readers. Oliver notes, however, that the ego-like, agent-like, substantialist view of the self which has characterized Western individualism has been undermined by the inability of this view to deal with non-Western views. It has also been largely responsible for the exploitation of nature by Western technology, and here Oliver makes common cause with Kohák's personalism. Oliver argues that "the imperialist posture of the West by which it purports to dominate world culture is a mirror image of the view of selfhood which underlies Western culture." He finds the roots of this Western notion of the individualized self in the philosophy of Augustine and Descartes where the substantial self was philosophy's point of departure. Its weakness, he argues, is the lack of a social view of the self. For that he turns to the tradition of mysticism in the West, especially Meister Eckhart; and to the tradition of Eastern Orthodox theology, in which God's will takes precedence over creature will; eternity takes precedence over time; and being is understood as communion. Drawing on the Kyoto school of Zen Buddhism, the mysticism of Meister Eckhart, Eastern Orthodox Christian theology, and the Jewish philosophy of Martin Buber, Oliver outlines the possibility of a new, global view of the nonself which overcomes the triumphalism of Western individualism.

Lawrence Cahoone counters with reflections on the limits of this social and rational notion of selfhood. He begins with a chilling and telling tale from James Clavell's *Shogun* in which a group of British sailors are captured by Japanese in the early seventeenth century, and made to draw straws to choose one of them to die. Boiled in a cauldron all night until he finally dies at dawn, the victim's screams elicit from the survivors the thought that "we are here, and he is there, and *it wasn't me.*" Cahoone notes that a number of philosophers have argued recently that rationality is inherently social. He concludes that if we take ourselves at some point to be irreducibly *asocial* — as in his illustration — then we are, in our asocial individuality, irreducibly irrational. It is the irrationality of the asocial self which Cahoone sets out to explore. He does not deny that the self's identification with others is necessary and virtually universal. But he argues that this identification does not exhaust the self, and that the self can and does at critical times judge the world from the point of view of its singularity. Here

Cahoone shares some common ground with Kohák, but none with Oliver, whose relationalism has no place for isolated singularity. Cahoone accepts the current identification of rationality with sociality, and he acknowledges that this does not make rationality a product of social convention but only a function of human interaction. Nevertheless, he points out an unforseen consequence: when we make judgments from that perspective, in which the difference between oneself and others is absolute, then such judgments are necessarily irrational. Further, the difference between social and asocial judgments is not rationally reconcilable. So Cahoone moves away from the tradition of Aristotle, Kant, Hegel, and the American pragmatists, and toward Kierkegaard and the existentialists. He takes Kierkegaard's *Fear and Trembling* as an illustration of his thesis. Kierkegaard points out that ethical judgments are both social and universal. As a result, they are rationally coherent and "fully disclosed" so there is no room for the idiosyncrasies and undisclosed "interiority" of unique, personal experience. For Kierkegaard *faith*, as the definitive event of individual interiority, therefore contradicts and transcends the ethical. So the central focus of *Fear and Trembling* is reflection on the story of Abraham's sacrifice of Isaac, in which faithful obedience to the commands of God transcends the rational ethic of a father's relation to his son. Cahoone argues that Kierkegaard is right "that the choice between identification with the community and the perspective for which the difference between oneself and others is absolute cannot be a rational one. . . ." Individual choice of this sort is *criterion-less*. It may well have a compelling cause, but not a reason. "There can be no *ought* in this case."

Edward James notes that the idea of the self in the Western tradition has been dominated by the mind/body dualism. His project is to sketch a holistic view of the self in which the either/or of dualism can be transformed by a both/and, through the notion of a *bounded continuum*, a unique interrelationship between two extremes, where the extremes interpenetrate, without excluding either one. Heat and cold is an example. On a continuum any particular point is more or less hot or cold. In regard to the mind/body continuum James wants to say "(1) that mind and body themselves are not independent substances but are instead poles of the mind/body continuum, (2) that as poles they are defined in terms of, and so are interdependent on, each other, (3) that there is no one or inclusive ordering of mind and body, but rather (4) mind and body merge or come together in an inexhaustible number of connections."

As illustration he takes the action theory problem of *going astray* — whether we can go wrong knowingly and willingly. Is the problem weakness? Weak people see what they ought to do, but do otherwise. But then we must speak of ourselves as having been overcome by a power greater than ourselves. Another way of understanding going astray is perversity. Perversity is a distortion of deliberation. It is to choose a course of action for some reason external to oneself — like deciding to be a physician because that is what my parents want me to be, and taking this to be what I really want for myself. At this point, James says, I am being perverse. The perverse are not divided against themselves as the weak are. They see themselves as rational, but what they are doing is not rational.

The third main account of going astray is to do evil. Here the self is not self-conflicted or perverse, but its "reasons" for doing evil are what James calls "antireason." While the rational paradox of going astray remains — it is not rational to do wrong knowingly, yet we do — James's argument is that "as a mind-body continuum the self can be held to be indirectly and so paradoxically responsible" since bodily desires and limitations mix with the mind's rationality in choosing our actions.

Our second section deals with selfhood in various cultures, beginning with Eliot Deutsch's essay "The Comparative Study of the Self." He notes at the outset that there are different understandings of selfhood within each cultural tradition. In the West, for example, the Greek *psyche*, the German *geist*, and the English *mind* all have distinctive meanings. There are some common presuppositions in each cultural tradition, however, and his essay explores ways in which each tradition can enlarge its understanding of selfhood by incorporating elements from other traditions. So Deutsch's essay is not only a study in comparative philosophy, it is an intercultural philosophy of the self.

Acknowledging that different traditions have different understandings of selfhood, and that even comparable problems will have different solutions in different cultures, Deutsch nevertheless argues that there is a "deep grammar" of human experience which all cultures share. Cultural difference makes comparative philosophy's initial task one of mutual understanding, but the common "deep grammar" of human experience allows for a second, creative role in which comparative philosophy appropriates various elements into one's own ground of thought and being. As an example of this approach Deutsch takes John Locke's philosophy of the self as outlined in his *Essay Concerning Human Understanding.* Locke defines a person in terms of self-consciousness, leading to the problematic conclusion that one is not responsible for an action if one is not conscious of having performed it. Deutsch notes that the difficulty arises because of the mind/body dualism which Locke presupposes. In the spirit of Edward James's idea of a bounded continuum, Deutsch notes that most Asian thinking presupposes some kind of mind-body unification. And in common with Kohák's personalism, he notes that Chinese thought sees a person as an achievement, not a mere given of nature. That continuing achievement involves appropriation of bodily as well as mental characteristics, giving the person a continuity over time which is lacking in Locke's analysis. Deutsch concludes that no one school of thought or tradition can provide conclusive answers to a philosophical problem as complex as selfhood. Problems in one tradition can be partially resolved, however, by the rich resources of other philosophical traditions.

John Carman's study of "The Dignity and Indignity of Service: The Role of the Self in Hindu *Bhakti*" begins by observing that, contrary to popular opinion in the West, there is a wide variety of conceptions of selfhood in Indian philosophy. His special interest is in that school of Vedānta philosophy which, unlike the nondualism associated with Śankara, emphasized singing and dancing and acting out what is called *bhakti,* devotion to a personal God in a community of devotees. His essay focuses on the work of Rāmānuja, especially a text which deals with the status of the "servant" of God. Carman earlier wrote in his *The Theology of Rāmānuja* that "God is the owner and master, and all His creatures are in the position of slaves." He is now persuaded, however, that Rāmānuja's view is more complex than he had at first thought, and that "service" has a characteristic dignity as well as indignity.

Carman comes to his new conclusion as a result of reevaluat-

ing the poetic form of a key verse in Rāmānuja's text. The relation
of the devotee to the Lord is analogous to the relation between
soul and body. "In the first part of the relationship the superior
reality supports all the inferior reality; the Lord underlies souls
as souls underlie their bodies. In the second part of the relationship, the superior reality controls the inferior one, and this is imagined as control from within; the soul *within* the body, and the
Divine 'Inner Controller' within the soul." But in the third part
of the relationship the body underlies the soul, thus having dignity in its service of the higher reality. Carman's analysis of this
text supports Deutsch's view of the integral relation between soul
or mind and body in much Hindu philosophy. For Carman's purposes, however, the text is even more significant in showing that
service of the Lord, and the community of devotees, is not simply
"slavish," but can have its own proper dignity.

Livia Kohn's specialty is ancient Chinese thought, and her
essay explores the role of spontaneity in Chinese views of selfhood.
She begins with a distinction between the "object self" and the
"observing self" which she takes from the psychologist Arthur Deikman. She finds parallels between this distinction and the one which
Taoist and Confucian thought makes between "selfhood" and "spontaneity." For Taoism this is the dichotomy between human beings
and the Tao, between a mind which is ego-centered and one which
is pure spirit, and between one's individual body and the body
of the cosmic order. Confucianism, on the other hand, distinguishes
between the ego-centered self and the fulfillment of roles determined by society; and a mind absorbed with individual desires
as opposed to a mind devoted selflessly and instinctively to one's
appropriate function in the world.

Deikman argues that the "observing self" transcends the motivation of the object self. "The path to that transcendence is service — real service, which means serving the task and, ultimately,
serving what mystics call the Truth." The "object self" thinks, feels
and acts in a self-affirming mode. But for Chinese thought there
is a higher mode of being in the world which includes elements
of thought and feeling but is receptive and spontaneous. This mode
has to be learned, and "object-dependent selfhood has to be adjusted, subdued, cultivated, or destroyed altogether." The *Daode
jing* argues that the true sage should put oneself in the background

and withdraw as soon as the work is done; and the *Zhuangzi* even announces, "The perfect man has no self!" This is the ethical foundation of the "no-self" doctrine which became prominent in Japanese Zen Buddhism, and which Oliver has further developed in his relational metaphysics. Kohn concludes that, in spite of significant differences, both Taoism and Confucianism "deny the limited ego of the object self and favor the wider openness of the observing self. They both strive for cultivating and subduing selfhood in favor of spontaneity."

Our final section deals with the problem of selfhood in theology, biology, psychoanalysis, and political theory. We begin with Krister Stendahl's reflections on "Selfhood in the Image of God." He is bemused by the fact that this powerful expression of our common humanity — since *all* people share in this image of God — has been long neglected, and he sets out to understand the sources of this neglect, and to discover the resources for overcoming it. He begins with the story of "the Fall" in the third chapter of Genesis. Like Oliver, he argues that Augustine has been instrumental in so emphasizing the doctrine of original sin that the operative idea of human beings as made in the image of God has been virtually cancelled. He cites Elaine Pagels's *Adam, Eve and the Serpent* in arguing that the early Christian tradition did not interpret the story in Augustinian fashion. Early Christianity read it as making the transition from innocence to responsibility, not from moral purity to original sin. Stendahl emphasizes the element of free will in the Genesis story, and notes whimsically that "human beings did not get a day unto themselves in the Genesis story of creation." Humans are rather participants "in a binding continuity with the whole creation."

The idea that our selfhood is to be understood primarily in terms of God's selfhood is emphasized in the Eastern Orthodox tradition. Stendahl, like Oliver, finds resources there for a holistic view of the self which contrasts with Augustine's dualistic one. Stendahl points out that the Western church tended to identify Christians as those who believed in Jesus Christ. In the Eastern church, however, a Christian is one who believes in the Holy Trinity. He faults both biblicists and liberals for a failure to incorporate this emphasis in recent theology. He argues that "the worship of the triune God is a liberation from that idolatry in which we picture

God in our own image." He notes especially that it liberates us
from the racial and gender prejudices of our culture. He also argues in a manner akin to Oliver's relationalism that the selfhood
of God is not some rarefied substance or even "person," but "an
ongoing relationship between the Father and the Son and the
Spirit." Our selfhood is modeled on this interdependence, giving
and receiving in constant mutuality. This requires a reevaluation
of the idea of love presented in Anders Nygren's influential *Agape
and Eros*. Stendahl finds Nygren's God too transcendent, and God's
agape therefore full of condescension. He counters, "But as I read
the Christian texts, I find that Jesus loved sinners because he really
liked them. He found something lovable in the sinner where others did not." And he concludes: "When I perceive God as that
insatiable, dynamic interrelationship, I find always that there is
something in God as a mystery which is beyond the sum total of
my little images."

Alfred Tauber's essay on "The Organismal Self in Its Philosophical Context" returns us to ground issues in philosophy by
examining biological ideas of organism in the work of Elie Metchnikoff, and relating them to developments in modern philosophy.
Metchnikoff revolutionized biology in 1884 with his view that immunity is an active process, and that the integrity of an organism
is not a given, but "an unceasing process of self-definition." For
Metchnikoff health now became a purposeful striving for harmony
within an organism's potentially disharmonious assembly of evolved
constituents. "No longer are the ancient humors in balance, but
life's cellular components are in conflict." This meant that health
is not a given, but an active achievement attained in conflict — or,
better, an achievement toward which the organism strives, since
Metchnikoff regards health as an idealized goal, not a norm. Rather,
disharmony was the norm, and harmonization the process whereby
the organism moved toward self-fulfillment.

Tauber notes that this vision reflected Metchnikoff's own psychology, since he was subject to severe depression. In relating Metchnikoff's views to the philosophies of William James and Friedrich
Nietzsche, he notes that both of them were also subject to comparable "nihilistic challenges." James's radical empiricism emphasizes that reality is an ever-changing flux, and that experience is
the result of attention to some aspect of that experience, accord-

ing to our needs and interests. "The self must thereby differentiate itself, and it does so only by active engagement." Tauber argues that the Metchnikovian self is reiterated in James's epistemology.

The same kind of dynamic view of selfhood creating harmony out of initial disharmony is found in Nietzsche's emphasis on the will to power. The self is actualized in its struggle. Tauber notes that Nietzsche's mature philosophy was taking shape at the same time that Metchnikoff was presenting his theory of immunity and James was at the midpoint of writing his *Principles of Psychology*. While there is no evidence that they directly influenced each other, Tauber is struck with the common task in which they were engaged. "The task for each is to create the self: Metchnikoff envisioned the organism striving for harmony amongst competing, disparate elements; James sought to place the individual in its particular context in a plenum of experience by selection and volition; Nietzsche's Zarathustra proclaimed man as becoming, striving to overcome himself and in the process of re-creation denying nihilistic destruction."

John Mack's "Psychoanalysis and the Self: Toward a Spiritual Point of View" deals with the values which undergird psychoanalytic practice. He proposes that a spiritual point of view is now required in order to understand the psyche more fully, and to interpret the conditions of contemporary human life. He points to a host of problems which have eluded treatment based on traditional, limited views of the psyche. They include addictive disorders, child abuse and other forms of domestic violence, and increased reliance on drugs. He also notes that many people are turning toward "holistic" or "alternative" therapies as a result of unmet hunger for spiritual elements in their treatment.

Definition of the *spiritual* is admittedly difficult because of the complexity of the idea and the inevitable subjectivity of any definition. He quotes Barbara Marx Hubbard on the wide spread of mystical experience in our time, but admits that most spiritual experience is less dramatic and more subtle. His point of departure is the realization that there is a realm of the numinous, "another reality beyond that which is immediately manifest to our sense or reason." Further, our world has design, even intention, and is not random flux or a chance creation. One difficulty with entering the spirit world, however, is the disturbing emotions, such as great fear or sadness, which are associated with that experience. Another is that we have not been educated in the language of spirituality, even though virtually all other peoples throughout history have experienced its central importance to their lives. He lists six elements of a spiritual point of view: an attitude of appreciation or awe toward the mysterious in nature; an openness to the cosmos as sacred; the application of a cosmological (non-materialist) perspective on reality; a subjective hesitancy, expressing consciousness of the mystery of being and dignity of every person; a distrust of all human institutions; and an attitude toward the emotionally troubled which is focused less on pathology, and more on the shared fate of what it means to be human.

Mack calls for a wider human identity in which our individual core self is connected to diverse others. The spirituality he proposes is therefore not one of personal inwardness alone. It is a principle of social interaction as well. The widespread phenomenon of mass death, and the ecological crisis of global survival, demand a new spirituality. Here Mack echoes the same call for selflessness-in-community which is characteristic of so many of our authors. "Human beings grow when, in the confrontation with death, they are enabled to discover a new personal perspective, sacrificing their egoism before it is the body's time to die."

We conclude with Bhikhu Parekh's examination of "The Liberal Discourse on Violence." His concern is not with philosophical *theories* of violence, but rather the way in which the issue is formulated and debated in such liberal democracies as Britain, France, and the United States. These liberal democracies all recognize the rule of law, civil and political liberties, constitutionally guaranteed basic rights, and a limited government based on internal checks and balances. What is distinctive about them, however, is that they take the individual as the ultimate unit of political life and organize their institutions around individuals. Parekh's thesis is that this individualism has limited our understanding of violence, and that the notion of the self which is basic to this individualistic analysis is not sufficiently social. As a result, there is much violence in liberal democracies which goes virtually unnoticed because it is structural or institutional, or not physically directed against any particular individual.

In a telling illustration Parekh notes that "if I push a drunkard into a puddle and he dies, I am responsible for his death because I intended and willed it and initiated a chain of events culminating in it. If he fell into it by accident or was pushed into it by someone else, I bear no causal and moral responsibility for his death. If I could have saved his life but did not, I bear no or only a minimum responsibility for his death." Parekh also notes that the liberal discourse on violence associates harm primarily with the physical body and, to a lesser extent, with damage to property. In the liberal discourse violence is also confined to deliberate human acts.

The situations which are distorted by the liberal view on violence can be illustrated by the situations of people in prison. "Prisoners are locked up in bleak cells, sometimes two and even three in a room not large enough for even one. . . . They are insulted, degraded, treated with contempt, and sometimes beaten up by other prisoners and even officers. . . . In fact, force is exercised in the spirit of violence and brutalizes both its agents and its victims." Parekh's conclusion is that we need to revise many of our individualist assumptions and develop more satisfactory conceptions of the individual, agency, causality, duty, negative action, and collective responsibility. He proposes that we should reverse the individualist schema and place the victim rather than the agent at the center of our inquiry. "Rather than ask *if* and *how* we are causally and morally responsible for physical harm to others, we should ask *why* millions suffer distress, injury, pain, and premature deaths, and what we could do to prevent and alleviate them."

Our authors have much in common. There is a broad emphasis among them on the social dimensions of selfhood, and the dynamic growth and change which characterizes the idea of a person as a project or a tentative achievement, rather than a static substance which is given. There is also much agreement that selfhood is a bodily concept as well as a mental one, and that a developed philosophy of the self must integrate mind and body in some functional way. Finally, the tendency toward holistic views of selfhood rejects the idea of a value-free world, and reaches toward the notion of a world of common human values. This emphasis, in turn, suggests that the web of relations in which individual selfhood develops is at least potentially a global community in which human selves have increasingly close ties with the earth's natural life, and the life of the cosmic order itself. Although their emphases and interpretations differ from one another on some not insignificant issues, there is broad agreement that the free-standing self of America's rugged individualism is gradually being socialized in response to the demands of an increasingly global community.

NOTES

1. Sarvepalli Radhakrishnan, *Indian Philosophy*, 2nd ed. rev. (London: George Allen & Unwin, 1929), vol. 2, p. 476.

PART I

Philosophies of Selfhood

Selves, People, Persons:
An Essay in American Personalism

ERAZIM KOHÁK

IN THE NAVAJO TALES of the creation, the *Dineh* – or "the People," as the Navajo refer to themselves – make a rather late appearance. Other people come before them. There are the Beetle People and the Insect People; there are important persons such as Hosteen Badger, Hosteen Bear, Hosteen Snake, who is a special friend of the Navajo, and of course the Coyote, the trickster who scattered the blanket full of stars to make the Milky Way. It was the Coyote who brought on the flood that destroyed the third world by stealing the Water Person's baby and hiding it under his cloak. In the fourth world, he would marry a beautiful Navajo maiden and come to live in her hogan. . . .

A coyote wearing a cloak? Marrying one of the People and living in a hogan? What is going on here? Is the Coyote really a coyote or is he a person? The traditional Navajo do not ask the question. Of course the Coyote is both. In their world, there are many kinds of persons, of whom some are humans and others are not, and their transactions are always transactions among persons. It is only we, humans of the Western cultural heritage, who have convinced ourselves that only members of our own species can claim the status of persons and the respect due them while all other being is no more than raw material that we can use or abuse at will. Perhaps it is because we have forgotten what it means to be a person.

I want to explore a philosophical tradition which does not take the concept of being a person for granted, that of American personalism. I do not wish to present a list of personalist doctrines and argue for their truth. Rather, bracketing the question of truth,

17

I want to philosophize in the spirit of personalism, trying to see the world through personalist eyes. In the process, I shall suggest that we think of being a person not as a matter of belonging to the species *homo sapiens sapiens*, but rather as a task to which we are called. Second, I shall suggest that being a person is not an exclusively human mode but rather a fundamental metaphysical category, and that there are sound reasons for thinking of reality as a community of persons. Finally, I shall suggest that within the community of persons humans have a special task and a special responsibility that define the distinctively human way of being persons.

I shall not, in the end, remove the brackets and ask whether the personalist conception of the place of humans in the cosmos is in some sense "true." That is never an appropriate question about a metatheoretical conception which, by definition, is compatible with any state of the universe whatever. Instead, I shall suggest that the personalist conception of the cosmos and of the place of humans therein is a legitimate one and, for good and sufficient reason, preferable to its more familiar alternatives.

The term *personalism* was introduced into American philosophic discourse by a Boston University professor, Borden Parker Bowne—the author whom William James most often quotes when, in his *Principles of Psychology*, he calls upon the testimony of philosophy. A pupil of the German Kantian Hermann Lotze, Bowne found in the concept of *person* the category that would enable him to resolve the problems of the place of moral subjects in a material world, posed in his day in the long-forgotten terminology of "faith and science." Bowne's personalism remained the dominant mode of thought at Boston University for some three generations. It was carried on and elaborated first by Edgar Sheffield Brightman, a persistent inquirer into questions of metaphysics and morals, and most recently by Peter Anthony Bertocci, my own older colleague, mentor, and friend, whose interests reached to theology and psychology. It is in their spirit—though not necessarily in their idiom—that I want to reflect on the meaning and uses of being a person.

In the beginning, there is the recognition that being a person is not a fact but a task—or, perhaps, the terminological decision to use the word *person* to designate a mode of being of which we are capable and to which we are called but which, the American personalists would have added, God alone fully exemplifies. That, today, may have a dated ring, though the insight it seeks to articulate seems to me not at all dated. At its core, it is the recognition, echoed subsequently by existential philosophers, that being born into the species *homo sapiens sapiens* does not of itself sufficiently determine our being. It is, at most, a start, a chance to become who we shall be, and that process is not automatic or its outcome certain. A dog cannot be in-dog or a horse in-horse, but a human can be in-human: our humanity is a possibility of which we can fall short.

The American personalist chose to reserve the term *person* for this normative sense of our humanity. The reasons for the choice, to be sure, were largely fortuitous. The rhetoric of the American 1890s abounded in references to a "personal God" and to God "as person." Yet the norm the personalists sought was not a culturally determined one, like the conception of the *homo humanus* of ancient Rome, the gentleman of Victorian England, or even Aristotle's man of virtue — whose virtues, however admirable, sound very culture-specific today. Rather, they were looking for a possibility that is intrinsic to the being of humans — literally, to the way that humans *be* — simply as human, and which is yet a possibility whose realization is not automatic but confronts humans as a task.

Today, such an effort may well appear vain from the start, a remnant of the Enlightenment illusion that a culture-free articulation of our culture-bound humanity is possible. Certainly, humans have always and everywhere recognized the distinction between the *sein* and the *sollen* of their humanity, between what they are and what they ought to or might be. It might even be possible to argue that, for all the diversity of terminology, they have reached a general consensus as to what they are, as finite, conscious, incarnate freedom. When, however, they attempted to articulate the *sollen*, the normative vision of humanity, they have invariably described a distinctly culture-specific ideal dominant in this or that culture. In fact, when we read, for instance, Peter Bertocci's noble, sensitive, and perceptive descriptions of what it means to be truly a *person*, it is difficult not to be very much aware that they were written in America in the 1950s.

And yet, in spite of the very dated idiom, we catch glimpses

of a different vision, as when Bertocci introduces his poetic metaphor of fixing our vision on a distant star, or when Bowne, com-
piling a list of "human needs" after the manner of turn-of-the-
century psychology, places the need for truth at the head of the
list. There are enough such glimpses of universal humanity to war-
rant suspending our disbelief to hear the personalist question:
What is the possibility of being human which is intrinsic to our
being but which yet confronts us as a task? What does it mean
to be a *person?*

Perhaps etymology can suggest a starting point, as long as
we turn to it in a spirit of whimsy rather than of Teutonic seri-
ousness. Before Christian theology burdened the word with every
manner of theological freight, *persona* referred simply to an actor's mask which the actor put on to signal to the audience that
he or she was assuming a role, and what role he or she was assuming. So, initially, *persona* is a role, and we can start out with the
supposition that to be as a person means first of all *having a role.*
Metaphors, to be sure, do not run on four legs, and ours should
not be expected to do so. In speaking of being a person as *having
a role,* I do not mean to suggest that all the world's a stage, or
that the play has an Author and we are cast into a role, possibly
by the three Fates, at our cradle. Nor do I mean to preclude such
a possibility. I wish to bracket all such considerations rigorously
and single out only one specific aspect of the metaphor: that to
be as a person means to *have a role,* to have an agenda of one's
own and one's own distinctive style as we go busily and purposefully
about that agenda.
An impersonal — or better, a nonpersonal — being would then
be one which had no agenda of its own, a being passively driven
to and fro by every wind of chance, willing nothing, seeking nothing, drifting aimlessly like a wind-blown leaf. It would be a being that had no agenda — and no *style* of its own, looking to the
world to shape the way it went about being. Mixing our metaphor
atrociously, it would be like a wind-blown leaf reading a fashion
magazine to learn what color to turn this fall. Definitely, being
a person must include minimally having an agenda of one's own,
going about purposefully building up a distinctive life in a distinctive way.

Traditional personalists stressed a corollary: a person is a unitary, self-consistent being, with a series of desirable personal traits, from consistency in thought and deed to a rejection of lying, since a conscious lie represents a destructive split in a subject's consciousness and personality. In their exhortations, they presented a noble virtues ethic which compares rather favorably with recent attempts at moral dilemma resolution. For our purposes, though, another corollary may be more relevant — that a person, a unitary being with its own agenda, is a being who lives in a value-laden, meaningfully ordered world.

This appears to me crucial. For a being who is actively present in the world, with an agenda of its own, the world can never be value-neutral. It could be that to a nonpersonal being, a being who simply is, blown hither and yon by the winds of chance. That is a condition we at times approximate when stunned by a blow of fate or of a baseball bat, when our agenda collapses and there seems no point in anything. When we have no agenda, the world around us, too, appears pointless, indifferent, not a world of good and evil but one that is simply there, pointless and meaningless.

Yet for us, as human beings, that is always at most an approximation. For as living beings we are never wholly without an agenda. Even the very modest agenda of breathing, of inhaling oxygen and exhaling carbon monoxide, orders the world and endows it with value qualities. Airy places, rich in green plants, are good; dark dank dungeons bad and undesirable. Perhaps on some rarefied level of reflection we may not judge them so, but that is not how we experience them. Long before we reflect upon it, we encounter the world as meaningfully structured and value-endowed simply by virtue of our living presence therein. In relation to us the world is never indifferent. It is, necessarily and from the start, a world of good and evil, as it fosters or hinders the agenda of our being.

Nor is it simply a matter of immediate utility. Having an agenda also means having expectations. They may be wholly tacit, built into the structure of our being. But they mean that we encounter our world not as simply there but as living up to or falling short of our expectations. In addition to its value of utility, the world presents itself to us also laden with the value of relative perfection. Just as utilitarian ethics builds on the primordial experi-

ence of the world as fostering or hindering our agenda, so formal-
istic ethics builds on the no less primordial experience of the world
as more or less perfect. To be as a person means not only having
an agenda but also living in a value-laden, meaningfully ordered
world, a world of good and evil.

For a person-type being, one who persists through time, its
moments unified by an agenda, living in a value-laden world has
another consequence. Such a being remembers and anticipates,
and the flux of experience is not indifferent to it. Such a being can
cherish the good in its transient finitude, and it can grieve its pass-
ing. Being a person means being able to cherish the goodness of
the first trillium amid the spring moss, damp with melting snow,
and to grieve the pointless waste of the small furry creature crushed
by a heedless motorist. Having an agenda means caring; being able
to grieve and to cherish means being able to respect. A person is
a being who can grieve, cherish, and respect, caring in a world
of good and evil.

And, finally, since a person is a being who lives in a world
which is not indifferent, value-neutral, its own acts are not indifferent. If we may press yet another metaphor into service, we could
say that a person is a being who *plays by rules*. A nonpersonal
being might be present in the world as blind force or sheer inertia.
A personal being with an agenda amid a world of good and evil,
able to cherish, grieve, and respect, is constrained in its acts. Its
presence in the world is not arbitrary but has its appropriateness.
We might say, with Gary Snyder, that a personalist ethics is rooted
in etiquette, in respectful demeanor toward others and oneself —
or, borrowing yet another phrase, in treating persons, whether in
myself or others, ever as an end, not a means merely.

Out of such images a composite image of what it means to
be a person begins to emerge. It means having a role, a consistent
agenda and style. It means living in a value-laden world of good
and evil which demands respect. It means cherishing and grieving, and it means playing by rules.

To be sure, these are images, metaphors which resist all attempts at rigorous definition. If we were to attempt to reduce them
to an exact closed system, they would break down. Yet life itself
is an open system, and mathematical precision is seldom the point.

Far more often, the pressing task of philosophy is to generate images, metaphors capable of guiding action. The personalist conception of life as a growth to the full stature of being a person certainly did that. In part because the personalists did not strive for a mathematically precise conceptual system but offered open metaphors, their conception could be extended to psychology, to educational philosophy, to ethics, and could provide a plausible vision of the task of being human.

For consider, is not the common trait of all whom we regard as needing to be educated, as well as of those whom we regard as needing to be healed, that they are without an agenda, adrift in a world where good and evil are random, unable to cherish it or grieve for it? Are they not humans who never grew to the full stature of being persons, or whose project of being as persons collapsed?

They may be simply young. Young people on the threshold of life often have not had time to sort out their options and to focus their lives on an agenda. An education that provides them technical skills but lets them drift as persons in the vague hope that somehow they will "find themselves" does them little favor. The personalists with their conception of nurturing people to become persons challenged students actively to think through the options and implications of the human venture in life, in marriage, in religion, in ethics, building up a personality and an agenda. In its personalist decades — roughly the first six decades of this century — Boston University justly enjoyed the reputation of being a nurturing, not just a teaching, school.

The personalist vision could extend no less to the tasks of healing, as it did in Peter Bertocci's work in psychology. For again, is not the common ground of mental and existential disturbance precisely the collapse of personal agenda and style, of the project of one's life? Its proximate cause may be a failure of confidence, justified or unjustified, or a collision with an unyielding reality. But the result is an injured human being, without a sense of an agenda, without a sense of the goodness and badness of the world, literally adrift in a world in which nothing matters, too stunned to cherish or grieve, all rules seeming arbitrary. The personalist vision provides an agenda for healing: helping that human grow into the full stature of a person — finding a distinctive agenda and style, becoming sensitive to the world as a place of good and evil, learning to cherish, grieve, and respect.

At the same time, the personalist vision of humans as called to the task of becoming persons provided the Boston personalists with a sharp tool of social critique. It is not an accident that Martin Luther King, Jr., shaped his agenda in the matrix of Boston personalism, or that Boston University in its personalist decades was a source of social ferment. The personalist vision of society as the context whose task it is to nurture humans to the full stature of persons provided a standard which enabled the personalists to point out the many ways our society falls short of this vision not only in its failures but precisely in its vaunted achievements. A society whose sole agenda is continually to increase the personal consumption needed to fuel an ever-expanding economy which would provide a still greater personal consumption *ad infinitum adque nauseam* — while the homeless sleep on grates, and schools and hospitals crumble — does not nurture people to become persons. Not only the victims but also the affluent suffer. Humans can stand a great deal of meaningful deprivation but little meaningless affluence. The affluent seldom have a distinctive agenda. They have it all already, and care for none of it. Not knowing what to want, they want it all, and want it now. Their world of meaningless affluence is not a world of good and evil, but a world of boredom. It does not teach its people to cherish, grieve, and respect, but only to waste and consume. The personalists could challenge the commercialized version of the American Dream with the dream of Martin Luther King, Jr., the vision of society committed to making persons, not money, fueling its economy by investing in social justice.

The personalist *Bildungsphilosophie* and social critique proved so attractive that they tended to displace the metaphysical foundations of personalism, with unfortunate results. Ironically, the success of the personalist social agenda may be a great part of the reason why personalism as a distinctive philosophic option has largely faded from the American intellectual scene.

Yet the roots of personalism were distinctly philosophical. For Borden Parker Bowne, *person* was in the first place the basic metaphysical category, not simply an anthropological or a social one.

Though the categories of turn-of-the-century idealism in which Bowne elaborated that basic device may seem quaint today, the thesis itself has lost none of its relevance.

What is at stake, in the first place, is an insistence on the irreducibility of subject being in the economy of the cosmos, or, in more familiar idiom, the irreducibility of first-person categories to third-person ones. Had Bowne been writing in German, he might have said that "Dasein ist immer jemeinig." As it was, he insisted that *person*, as he used that term, is never an object, an entity, or *a* being, used as a substantive. It describes a distinctive mode of being present in the world, an activity which constitutes the world as meaningfully ordered.

"The world," we should stress, refers not to a collection of entities, but, in a usage that comes more easily in German than in English, to a coherent, ordered context, or more specifically to the mode of ordering characteristic of that context. "Meaningful ordering" then refers to relations which are essentially subject-related. In another place, I have described such relations as the relations of "near and dear": the relation "A is nearer than B" or the relation "A is dearer than B" is essentially one related to a subject and so, in our usage, a *meaning* relation. By contrast, the relation "A is 30 cm distant from B" refers to the measuring subject only accidentally. Essentially, it is an extensional relation, not a meaning relation. The life world of subject beings, Bowne is asserting, is essentially meaningfully ordered, and that ordering is a reality *sui generis*, not reducible to extensional ordering.

That is the fundamental distinction to which Bowne points with his contrast between "personal" and "impersonal" being. His personalistic contemporaries on the continent — Max Scheler in *Die Stellung des Menschen im Cosmos* or Edmund Husserl in *Ideen II*, in which he adopts explicitly personalistic terminology — started from a tripartite distinction, speaking of inanimate, animate, and personal or *geistig* modes of being. That distinction, though, reflects three kinds of entities more than three modes of being. When we think in terms of the latter, as Husserl in *Ideen II*, the continuity of animate and personal being stands out: it is being in a meaningfully ordered world, a world of near and dear, sharply distinct from being in a merely extensionally ordered context.

When Bowne speaks of *person* as a basic metaphysical cate-

gory, he is asserting minimally that subject being—being constituting the world as a context of meaningful relations and com-
porting with respect to it as so constituted—is not reducible to the
extensional mode of being. The relationship "nearer than" is not
a variant of the relationship "30 cm distant"; nor is it a "subjective
reflection" of it in the mirror of *res cogitans*. It is not "merely subjective": A is nearer to me than B *in the world*, as a matter of fact,
not of opinion. But neither can it be said to be "objective" in the
popular sense, a relationship in an extensional world of Cartesian
res extendes. The Cartesian dichotomization collapses. The relationship "nearer than" is a real relationship in a meaningfully ordered world, subject-relative but not "subjective," and it cannot
be accommodated in a world of *res extendes* or in its counterpart,
the *res cogitans*.

Let me emphasize, as Bowne himself does not: we are not
claiming that subjects constitute their world as meaningful by "interpreting" it in reflective judgments, which is the usual claim of
subjective idealism. Rather, we are pointing out that subjects constitute the world as meaningful by their mere purposive presence,
even prior to and independently of any conscious reflection. As
we had noted earlier, while speaking of persons as beings in a world
of good and evil, simply my presence as a breathing being constitutes some places as more and others as less desirable. More
broadly, my mere presence as a purposive incarnate being constitutes some beings as nearer, others as dearer, than other beings.
The process, to be sure, continues in reflection, but when I first
begin to reflect, I do so already in the context of a world meaningfully ordered in virtue of my presence.

This is why the distinction between animate and *geistig* beings is not significant. It is not simply those persons who are human
and so reflect and discourse, but all subject beings, who by their
purposive presence constitute the world as meaningfully ordered
and value-laden. The grass is never an indifferent *res extensa*; simply
because there are woodchucks, grass is also *good*, fodder for the
creatures of the forest, meaningful and value-laden in relation to
subject beings. Grass as *res extensa* is never an experienced reality
but an abstraction, a construct. Though we may become aware
of the meaningful ordering—or, in Husserl's terms, of the "subjectivity" of the *Lebenswelt* ("life's world")—first as meaningful

ordering for human subjects, it is more basic than that, the *absolut fungierende Subjektivität* of the world of subject beings. In Bowne's terminology this is the personal world, the world of beings who are in the mode of persons.

Bowne is asserting minimally the irreducibility of the world of persons and of personal being to an objective world of *res extendes*. Though the subject beings who constitute the world as meaningful may have emerged in the course of evolution from a merely extensional, inorganic world, they cannot be reduced to it. Meaningful transactions represent a reality *sui generis* and cannot be explained as variations of extensional interactions.

That, though, is the minimal claim, and Bowne advances a stronger claim as well, asserting not only the irreducibility of subjectivity to objectivity, in a refurbished version of Cartesian dualism, but also the reducibility of objectivity to subjectivity. His personalism is an idealism.

Here it behooves us to tread with extreme care. Though Bowne's texts, such as *Metaphysics* or *Theory of Thought and Knowledge*, are at times less than unambiguously clear, what he is arguing is not a revival of a Fichtean idealism, of mind positing matter. We are not speaking of the extensional existence of entities in space-time, but rather of the ordering of the world in terms of meaning relations, intrinsically subject-related, as against conceiving of the world as ordered in terms of extensional relations among objects. Bowne's claim is not that thought gives rise to matter — except in the primordial sense of God creating the world — but rather that the description of the world as extensionally ordered does not represent a "discovery" of the world's "true reality" but rather an abstraction from its meaningful ordering. This abstraction is legitimate and useful for certain purposes, but it is in no sense primordial.

The point is that as experienced the *universum* is always and *ab initio* a personal world, meaningfully ordered. Its impersonal ordering, as we construct it in abstraction, can be reduced to a meaningful one: extension to the act of measuring. Objectivity is an intersubjectively constituted construct, legitimate as a special case theory, as one possible way of constituting the world as intelligible. Not reality, but objectivity, one way of conceiving of it, is reducible to subjectivity.

Furthermore, because *person* in Bowne's usage does not designate an individual subject but rather the mode of being of any and all possible purposive subjects — Brightman in one passage speaks of the personhood of the mosquito — Bowne's personalistic idealism is not a subjective idealism. The meaningful ordering of the world does not refer to the private preference of a particular subject but rather to the purposive presence of subjects as such. In that sense, Bowne's personalistic idealism is far more kin to Husserl's transcendental idealism as Husserl develops it in the third section of the *Krisis* and in the monadological texts of his *Nachlass* (Hua 15.526–662).

Marginally, we might note that the standard criticism raised against that position as Husserl presents it — implicitly by Heidegger, explicitly by Patočka — is that by interpreting objectivity as constituted within subjectivity it loses sight of what Nicolai Hartman called *die Härte des Realen* ("the recalcitrance of the real"). In Bowne's personalistic version of transcendental idealism, theism is the basic defense against such a criticism. Though it is within consciousness that the *universum* is constituted as the meaningful life world of persons and though objectivity is one dimension of that constitution, the *universum* remains God's creation. Its grounding in the transcendent God means that it always remains also other, irreducible to its constitution by created subject. Though subjects make it immanent in their being as the life's world, the world also remains transcendent, as God is also transcendent. Whether that is a viable solution or not, it did satisfy Bowne and his followers, so that the question of the autonomy of reality never became as prominent in personalist discussions as it did in post-Husserlian phenomenology.

Our present concern lies in a different direction. We have suspended the question of "truth" in the sense of asking whether personalism presents a true picture of reality. We are inquiring instead on a metatheoretical level — whether it provides an adequate root metaphor in Paul Ricoeur's sense, a fruitful intelligibility matrix in terms of which to orient our comportment. About such an intelligibility framework it is bootless to inquire whether it "corresponds" to what there is. A metatheory is in principle compatible with any state of the universe whatsoever and, conversely, the universe can be fitted within any metatheoretical framework, within one which takes a Cartesian extensional reality as its basic metaphor as well as within a personalistic one.

Still, the choice of intelligibility frameworks is not arbitrary because it is not simply a question of explanation. The way we choose to understand our world also affects the ways we comport ourselves with respect to it and the considerations which shall appear as relevant to our transactions with it. An extensional model and a personalistic model may have the same explanatory power but entail very different rules of comportment.

Very briefly, the only considerations relevant to the interaction of extended objects are those of force and inertia. As Thomas Hobbes already saw, if we conceive of all beings, including subject beings, as ultimately extended objects, we can account for their behavior — Drs. Watson and Skinner do it very nicely — but their interactions and our interactions with them will be governed only by the ethics of Thrasymachus and the politics of Chancellor Bismarck. For the purposes of human interaction, that is an option so clearly undesirable that we have routinely — if inconsistently — made an exception for the members of our clan, our cultural community, or, more recently, of our species. However, the rules of interaction entailed by the extensional mode of reality are seriously deficient in our dealings with nonhuman subjects as well. If we consider other species, plants, minerals simply as extended objects of various complexity but of no greater dignity, then our comportment toward them need be governed by no considerations other than those of force and inertia, perhaps tempered mildly by considerations of utility and squeamishness: we keep the horror of factory farming and animal experimentation carefully out of sight. For in recent centuries, that is how we have chosen to regard reality. The consequence is the wholesale destruction of the nonhuman world in the name of "Man's" conquest of nature, which we are now seeking to temper in the names of utility and sensitivity. Yet Heidegger points out the ultimate conclusion: in a world reduced to the status of extended objects, of raw material whose sole role is to satisfy human desires, humans find themselves "enframed" — in his word — in the complex of available raw materials. A world conceived of solely as consumable leaves humans with no role but that of the consumers. Whatever the explanatory power of the extensional model — the assumption that all beings are, ultimately, Cartesian *res extendes* — that is a high price to pay.

The personalists may well argue that the personal model has no less explanatory power for the purposes of the natural sciences. In the terminology of another era, the natural sciences are "special" sciences, dealing not with reality as such but with a special aspect of that reality, bracketing out all else. Very simply, a physicist studying the free fall of a body brackets out the fact that it is a living human body. Her sole interest is in rate of acceleration. She may be doing it for a noble purpose — say, designing more efficient parachutes — but, as a scientist, she brackets out her knowledge that this is the body *of a person.* That knowledge does not limit her ability to explain its free fall. Recognizing the *person*-al status of all animate beings, or of all beings, would affect the explanatory power of natural science no more than recognizing the *person*-al status of all humans. The brackets are securely in place.

However, a shift from an extensional to a personalistic conception of reality would represent truly a Kuhnian paradigm change with respect to the way we comport ourselves in our transactions with the world. For if reality is ultimately "a community of persons," in another of Bowne's phrases, then not only categories of force and inertia, but also categories of respect become relevant. If the slogan "Animals are small persons in fur coats" is not just a slogan but a recognition that animals are meaning-oriented subject beings, constituting the world as a context of good and evil, capable of rejoicing and suffering and worthy of respect, not "biomechanisms," then the routine procedures of our "agribusiness" and our research laboratories are an unspeakable moral monstrosity. The same will be true of the way we treat our forests, our rivers, our oceans, and the demands we make upon them. Even the most superficial glance at the self-destructive dynamics of our consumer civilization and our devastated planet, wasted more by senseless consumption than by careful use, makes the point. While the pure explanatory power of an extensional and of a personalistic paradigm may be analogous, the practical consequences of the latter are vastly superior.

At this point, though, we need to face a different question. The personalist paradigm extends the Kantian moral law from humans to all beings: "So act as to treat all beings, whether in your own person or that of another being, as an end and not as a means merely." Yes, humans are or can be persons, but there are also other persons to consider: the Beetle People, Hosteen Badger, the tree persons, and the humble "dormant monad," the boulder. If that is the case, how is differential action possible at all?

Here we are encountering what we might call the paralysis of universal compassion. A mouse must die that an owl may live. Traditional societies have solved the problem by relying on a hierarchical ordering so embedded in tradition as to appear natural. The traditional Navajo, with an exceptionally keen sense of the goodness of being and the evil of death, saw it as a part of the role of the mule deer to make a successful hunt, giving up its body to sustain the hunter. The role of the hunter is to accept that great gift reverently, taking no more than needed for sustenance. To waste a precious gift is deeply immoral. Less poetically but still analogously, medieval Europe, committed to the proposition that "esse qua esse bonum est," avoided the paralysis of compassion by relying on a hierarchical conception of reality, from God and the angels down to the humblest of God's inanimate creatures. A conception of reality as value-laden can avoid the paralysis of compassion only by relying on a conception of a hierarchical ordering.

For the modern age, however, the idea of a hierarchical ordering has become deeply problematic. Social change has become far too rapid for any hierarchical ordering to become so embedded in tradition as to appear simply "natural." All hierarchy has come to appear arbitrary. Ours is an egalitarian age. Yet respect for the integrity and intrinsic worth of all being, combined with an egalitarian conception of reality, inevitably leads to the paralysis of compassion.

Perhaps that is why the spread of the conception of reality as value-free and merely extensionally ordered parallels the rise of egalitarianism. The West in effect resolved the paralysis of compassion by abolishing compassion. A sixteenth-century Spanish physician, Gomez Pereira, solved Spain's moral dilemma concerning the genocide of the Taíno Indians in the Caribbean by teaching that beings who are not baptized Roman Catholics, be they trees, animals, or Indians, have no immortal soul and so no feelings and are entitled to no respect. That was the doctrine popularized a century later by a French soldier-of-fortune who felt no qualms about pillaging the Protestant, and so presumably soul-less, Bohemia in 1620, René Descartes. Action is possible because no being has any but extensional qualities.

The personalists, committed to a conception of the universe as value-laden, turned to the conception of personality to provide a hierarchical ordering and make action possible. All beings are persons in the minimal sense of having an integrity of their own and so of being worthy of respect. In that sense, humans must take moral categories into account in all their transactions. No being is so devoid of worth that it could be thoughtlessly wasted. All action requires moral justification, and heedless waste is always immoral. That is the egalitarianism of conceiving the world as a community of persons. There is no sphere of activity exempt from moral categories.

However, while all beings are persons in that minimal sense, not all beings live out the full range of personality. Only God can be said to be a Person fully, devoid of all passivity, of all indifference, of all contradiction, of all arbitrariness — whether we think of God as a living real presence or as an ideal limit. A boulder, at the other end of the scale, is only most minimally a person, just enough so that dynamiting it requires moral justification, no more. All other beings have their place on the scale between them. Plants or shellfish, though lacking a central nervous system, yet have an agenda of their own, a life they seek to pursue and so a world of good and evil. Conscious higher vertebrates — coyotes, chimpanzees, humans — are very fully persons, with a full range of personality which includes the ability to cherish and grieve, to hope and remember, to respect and play by rules. Though the difference in scope of personality does not justify indifference, it does justify differential choices, though always with respect and even reverence.

But by that criterion can humans claim a privileged standing among coyotes, chimpanzees, or dolphins? None of the personalist writers doubted that for a moment, or even raised the question. Theirs was an age of behaviorism in animal psychology and of confidence in progress in the wonderful works of "Man." Were we simply reporting their views, we would need only note

their confidence in the superiority of humans, based on the richness of their personality, their development of culture, and the
works of progress guaranteeing them a pride of place.

Today that assumption seems no longer self-evident. We have
become far less dogmatic, far more sensitive observers of our nonhuman kin. On all the evidence available to me, I would find it
rather difficult to sustain the claim that human personality or tem-
perament are in any way superior to those of the coyote, the chim-
panzee, or the beaver. As to the vaunted works of progress, they
appear highly problematic. We have placed an immense strain upon
the resources of the earth and are inflicting major irreversible damage upon it. We have rendered major portions of our globe unin-
habitable. Is the earth really better off for the presence of the human
species upon it?

Here I find myself going beyond the explicit writings of the
American personalists, though not without their help. The difference between humans and other higher vertebrate species seems
to me a negative one. What humans lack is a clear place and task
within the economy of the world. Beavers belong as an intrinsic
part of their ecosystem. Humans, borrowing a term from biology,
are an *exotic* species, one displaced from the habitat to which it
is adapted. We have moved from a natural to a cultural environment; or, in a terminology the personalists would have found familiar, we have moved from natural necessity to moral freedom.
Being a beaver is a fact; being human is a task. Other species do
not have to justify their existence. Humans do.

This is a tall order. Humans are far and away the most ex-
pensive species upon the face of the earth. What can they contribute? The works of progress can hardly be considered a contribution to the well-being of the earth. But humans can bring
eternity into time. All other beings live entirely within time, their
present shaped by the immediate past and the proximate future.
Humans are the species capable of standing out of time, knowing
the eternal. Humans can know the true, honor the good, cherish
the beautiful. Humans are the beings capable of bringing a dimension of the eternal into time, the time which without them
would pass into oblivion as the generations of porcupines beneath
the old dam. To know the true, to honor the good, to cherish the

beautiful — when humans do that, they are justifying their presence on this earth. When they do not, the world would be better off left to the coyotes.

Thus far, we have noted three points. One was the personalist conviction that becoming a person, a being with its own agenda, living in a world of good and evil, capable of grieving, cherishing, and respecting, is a task to which humans are called. This, we said, was the basis of personalism's ethical and social agenda. Second, we noted that the personalists locate this task within a conception of the cosmos as a community of persons, meaningfully ordered and value-laden. Person, not *res extensa*, is the basic metaphysical category, so that moral considerations are applicable to all human dealings. Finally, we said that the ability to act out the full scope of personality is the criterion which the personalists offer for making differential choices.

Perhaps just one brief final question ought to be asked. Why call it "personalism"? The position we have been examining is hardly unique. It is, basically, a version of transcendental idealism in the tradition of Kant and the German Enlightenment. It has a number of parallels in recent and contemporary thought, in Husserl's transcendental phenomenology, in Patočka's asubjective dialectical phenomenology, and, for that matter, in the philosophizing of a number of environmental philosophers. What is to be gained by calling it personalism and bringing in the whole arcane terminology of being a person — while explaining at every step that the term does not mean what it seems to mean? At what point does loyalty to a tradition become counterproductive?

In the religiously sensitive context of turn-of-the-century United States, there was a good reason. The conception of a personal God was powerfully present in the philosophical discussion of the time. In making such assertions as that God is the only being who can be fully said to be a person, the personalists linked their conception of the normative way of being human to God, much as Karol Wojtyla does in his personalism. The personalist terminology and imagery thus served to make the point that this is not a subjective idealism, reducing reality to human thought. It is God's transcendence which gives God's creation an irreducibility of its own. Though the meaningful order of reality is subject-related, it is only constituted, not created, by human subjects. God as the ultimate Person guarantees both the meaningful order and the irreducible reality of the real. As for the religious personalists today, the terminology of *person* and *personalism* implied all that.

It would be rather problematic to claim that it still implies all that in the context of contemporary philosophical discussion. For the "me generation," the term *person* points less to transcendence than to a rather bad immanence, the immanence of the self-centered *I*. The connotations of the term *personal* are today distinctly subjectivistic, not transcendental. Husserl, who used explicit personalistic terminology in his *Ideen II*, written at the time of the First World War, dropped it twenty years later when he worked out the project of *Ideen II* as the transcendental phenomenology in *Krisis III*. Might we not be better advised to follow his example?

It can be done. The basic insights of American personalism can be and have been developed without recourse to personalist terminology. We can speak of the irreducibility of the meaningfully ordered life's world as constituted by the presence of subject beings without introducing the term *person*, and quite possibly communicate more effectively. We can speak of being human as a task of moral growth to freedom and responsibility, offer a *Bildungsphilosophie* and a social critique, without using the personalist imagery. We can speak of the intrinsic worth of all being, making moral considerations mandatory, and of a hierarchy of relative worth, making action possible, without speaking of beings as persons. Does that terminology add to the position?

I must confess that I do not know the answer. I am convinced that the personalists and personalism have a great deal to offer. I am not confident that the title *personalism* is necessarily a part of it.

The Relational Self

HAROLD H. OLIVER

There is no-self, and it is the relational self.

Is IT POSSIBLE for those of us who have been brought up in the West, with its ego-like, agent-like, substantialist self, to imagine selfhood without ego, agency, or substance? Would anything essential to selfhood be surrendered by this operation? What would be gained by it?

These questions set the agenda for this exploration of a relational view of selfhood offered as an alternative to the individualistic, egocentric view of the self that prevails in the West. The exploration is initiated by the conviction that there is currently in the West a crisis of selfhood brought about by the insufficiency of the traditional view to deal with the phenomenon of globalization, with its positive feature of bringing Western views into close touch with non-Western, and its negative feature of exploiting nature in the interests of Western technology. The imperialistic posture of the West by which it purports to dominate world culture is a mirror image of the view of selfhood which underlies Western culture. The self that has arisen to master nature seeks further to master world culture.

How did this state of affairs come about? What was the origin of the modern Western notion of the self that subliminally offers itself along with its technology and technologically-driven politics?

I. THE GENESIS OF THE WESTERN EGO

The modern West has inherited from its Christian antecedents assumptions about the self of whose origins it has not always been aware. It is my thesis that the Western view of the self is a vestige of the Augustinian self so evident in his *Confessions*. It has no true classical antecedents, so we may assume that the Augustinian self was a mutation *sui generis*. Attempts to trace it back to Paul in Romans have failed, having been proven unsuccessful by Krister Stendahl in his famous essay, "Paul and the Introspective Conscience of the West."[1] According to Stendahl, Augustine's "plagued conscience" became normalized in medieval Christendom, and was at the root of Luther's self-understanding. Luther's repristination of Augustine's gospel entailed the institutionalization of the Augustinian self in Reformation Christianity. It could even be argued that Luther's bold individualistic posture over against established Christianity is evidence of this self-assertive self. The words of Luther, "Here I stand, God help me," are strongly individualistic. However worthy the cause in which they were uttered, they ensured that Protestantism would be unthinkable apart from individualism and voluntarism.

Further reinforcement of this Augustinian legacy was provided by the origins of modern philosophy in the West. Descartes, considered its founder, determined that modern Western philosophy would primarily be inquiry in search of certainty. His Methodic Doubt was inspired by Augustine's *si fallor, sum*, and his formula of discovery, *cogito ergo sum*, was as individualized as that of the former. If we contrast his view of the "subject" with that of the Scholastics, we must conclude that Descartes invented the modern notion of the subject which has been pervasive in most Western philosophy. German idealism absolutized it; phenomenology struggled unsuccessfully to overcome it; existentialism enculturated it.

At least since the time of Hegel, the fundamental problem of Western philosophy has been the status of the "not-I," of the "other." Hegel resolved the issue by a dialectic in which Being in itself generated its "other" (Being for itself) which was then sublated in Being in and for itself. The Left Hegelians developed various versions of the problematic of "self" and "other"; Kierkegaard retreated to the "subjectivity" of *den Enkelte;* Marx grounded his social theory on the notion of "self-alienation."

Theunissen has argued that the major European philosophers of this century, Husserl, Heidegger, and Sartre, all defined "the other" as the "alien I."[2] Their "social ontologies" were essentially plagued by their understanding of the "other" as a variable of the "I." On the contrary, Buber offered a true alternative with his dialogical philosophy of I-Thou.

It is safe to say that there has been a subjectivist bias in Western philosophy, manifest in its persistent idealism. Theology has also reflected this bias, making it a ready candidate for existentialism after World War I. Most theologians of that era in one way or another viewed the issues in terms of what was called "the subject-object problem in theology." The influence of Kierkegaard was strong throughout this period in both theology and philosophy. More recently, Robert Bellah and his associates addressed what they regard as the spectre of individualism in American modern society. Noting that Alexis de Tocqueville in the nineteenth century "warned that some aspects of our character—what he was one of the first to call 'individualism'—might eventually isolate Americans one from another and thereby undermine the conditions of freedom," Bellah et al. stated that "the central problem" with which they are concerned is "the American individualism that Tocqueville described with a mixture of admiration and anxiety," adding that "it is individualism . . . that has marched inexorably through our history . . . and may have grown cancerous."[3]

Dissatisfaction with the prevailing view of the self in the West has prompted feminists to seek alternatives to what they regard as the oppressive male-dominated asocial view of the self which runs rampant through modern culture. Black theologians, as well, feel alienated from the values in the culture which are not commensurate with their experience—values which, in my opinion, are directly linked to individualistic aggressiveness and dominance. It would seem that modern Western society has no legacy of a proper "social" view of the self upon which to draw in addressing current pressing psychological and ecological issues. Thus, there is a crisis of "selfhood" in the West, with few viable solutions available.

II. REENVISIONING THE SELF:
SOME NEGLECTED RESOURCES

Despite its pervasiveness in the West, the Augustinian view of the self has not been without rivals. Many of the speculative mystical theologians in the West operated out of non- and indeed anti-Augustinian assumptions about experience — one of the most notable being Meister Eckhart. Furthermore, Eastern Christianity stands as testimony to a sustained legacy of Christian selfhood outside the influence of Augustinian theology. In considering these two traditions in some detail, I hope to show that they offer neglected options to which we could today turn with great profit.

A. The Eckhart Legacy

As interest in mysticism has grown in modern times, Meister Eckhart's legacy of sermons and lectures has received renewed attention. This Rheinland mystic and preacher of the fourteenth century may stand alone in Western Christendom in making due place in theology for the Christian doctrine of self-denial. To understand Eckhart's view of the self is to appreciate the paradoxical character of self-denial. Eckhart inverted Augustine's emphases on time and will, thus making available a completely different view of the self. Let us consider these inversions.

Being Rather Than Becoming

Eckhart was a preacher who presented his difficult notions in sermons rather than treatises, so that in setting forth his radicalized view of the self, we shall have recourse primarily to his sermons. In considering his priority of being over becoming, we learn most from his famous sermon on Matt. 5:3, which a modern editor has titled: "Blessed Are the Poor in Spirit." Eckhart bases his homily on the Matthaean version of the Beatitude, which includes the additional words, "in spirit," rather than the more economical account in Luke, where the contrast is between "poor" and "rich" *simpliciter*. Eckhart's argument turns on the verb "are," for — over against the Augustinian version which entails "becoming" poor — he wants to make the point that "poverty" is not a goal separated from the will, but must be an act unified with its intention. Since it is difficult to find a modern Western writer who correctly perceives what is at stake in Eckhart's non-Augustinian understanding, I turn to the exposition of it by the famous Japanese philosopher, Daisetz T. Suzuki:

Our spiritual discipline . . . consists not in getting rid of the self but in realizing the fact that there is no such existence from the first. The realization means being "poor" in spirit. "Being poor" does not mean "becoming poor"; "being poor" means to be from the very beginning not in possession of anything and not giving away what one has. Nothing to gain, nothing to lose; nothing to give, nothing to take; to be just so, and yet to be rich in inexhaustible possibilities — this is to be "poor" in its most proper and characteristic sense of the word, this is what all religious experiences tells [sic] us. To be absolutely nothing is to be everything.[4]

Lest it seem that Eckhart's is a later, mystical reading of this logion of Jesus, we should do well to consider a similar, but neglected logion: "For to him who has will more be given, and he will have abundance; but from him *who has not, even what he has will be taken away*" (Matt. 13:12). No logical, ordinary meaning can be given to the phrase "from him who has not, even what he has will be taken away"; it is as truly paradoxical as Eckhart's "being poor," and has the added feature of honoring the dialectic of emptiness-fullness in the *kenotic* tradition. As we shall see momentarily, a view of time and will quite different from Augustine's is propelling Eckhart's interpretation.

God's Will Rather Than Creature Will

In extolling the virtue of "disinterestedness" (*Abgeschiedenheit*), Eckhart allows the argument to pivot on the distinction between "God's will" and the "creature will." Contrary to Augustine's emphasis on the human will, Eckhart admonishes sublating the creaturely will into God's will:

As long as a person keeps his own will, and thinks it his will to fulfill the all-loving will of God, he has not the poverty of which we are talking, for this person has a will with which he wants to satisfy the will of God, and that is not right. For if he wants to be truly poor, he must be as free from his creature will as when he had not yet been born. For, by everlasting truth, as long as you will to God's will, and yearn for eter-

nity and God, you are not really poor; for he is poor who
wills nothing, knows nothing, and wants nothing.[5]

The difference between this and Augustine's admonition, "Love
God, and do as you will," should be obvious. It should be equally
evident that two different views of selfhood are entailed in these
differing conceptions of will.

Eternity Rather Than Time

At the root of the two preceding distinctions, between being
and becoming, and between God's will and creature will, is a view
of time radically different from Augustine's. Whereas Augustine
temporalized "the will" in such a way that the ego — whether that
of the "plagued conscience" or of the morally "superior" ego —
could emerge in the forced interval between intention and act,[6]
Eckhart "englobed the successiveness of man in the simultaneity
of eternity"— to adapt words which Baron von Hügel used of the
Gospel of John.[7]

In Eckhart's sermon to which the editor has assigned the apt
title, "Get beyond Time!" the Rheinland preacher distinguishes
between "God's day" and "the world's day." Whereas the latter
comprises astronomical time, God's day is "the real Now-moment."
He adds, "All time is contained in the present Now-moment." It
soon becomes apparent from this sermon that space is also implicated in this claim, so that we could speak of the Here-Now-
moment. He warns his hearers: "As long as one clings to time, space,
and quantity, he is on the wrong track and God is strange and
thus far away." Thus, God does not enter the emptiness willed by
the self, as though the self must "become empty"; "God does not
first need to enter the person who is already free of all otherness
and creature nature, because he is already there."[8] We could conclude that the self of self-denial is no-self; for if the self is the agent
of the denial, the denial is but a foil for self-assertion. Eckhart's
self is the no-self that is God's self.

With this Western example in place, we turn now to the notion of selfhood in Eastern Christianity which permits us access
to a non-Augustinian Christian tradition.

B. *Orthodox Christianity*

The Orthodox Tradition is a many-splendored legacy to which I cannot begin to do justice in the short compass of this essay. I shall focus on two features of its theology, the *perichoretic* interpretation of the Trinity, and *deification*.

Being as Communion:
The Perichoretic Interpretation of the Trinity

The term *perichoresis* sets the Orthodox interpretation of the Trinity apart from the one dominant in the West where the emphasis was placed upon *una substantia*. In the East the focus was upon the *tres personae*, or hypostases, to such an extent that it was often misunderstood as tritheism. John Zizioulas has recently shown how the perichoretic doctrine which interpreted the relation of the three persons of the Trinity as "mutual interpenetration" led to the notion of Being as Communion. It could be argued that *perichoresis* is a new philosophical category of relation which arose out of deep theological reflection. As a category, its meaning is "distinct, but not separate." It is a relational rather than a substantialist theory of reality like we find in the West, and has the essential feature of placing emphasis upon "personhood" rather than "substantial being." Accordingly, Eastern theologians interpreted the three persons of the Trinity as "distinct, but not separate."[9] They properly resisted the addition of the *filioque* clause to the Nicene Creed which had been polemically inserted by the West, because the Orthodox realized the threat it posed to their perichoretic interpretation.

Deification as Relational Personhood

The bearing of this *perichoretic* doctrine of the Trinity upon the Eastern view of selfhood was such as further to widen the gulf between East and West. In one sense, the relation of self and God was interpreted *perichoretically*, that is, as distinct but not separate; hence the Eastern term *theosis*, "deification." The difference between East and West with respect to the relation of humanity to God is especially evident in the different meanings each assigns to the *imago dei*. Whereas in the West, the Fall means the loss of the quality of goodness shared with the deity in creation, in the East the loss does not annul the true likeness that we share in God's glory. As one Orthodox scholar phrased it:

> While the West, from St. Augustine onwards, has been chiefly preoccupied with what is in *man* which allows him to receive God, Eastern theology is concerned mainly with establishing what is in *God* which makes Him give Himself to man.[10]

This claim is taken a step further by the late Orthodox theologian, Nissiotis: "Man, then, is not to be defined by his sin, by his state of bondage, but in relation to his end in Christ and the work of the Paraclete in him."[11] It is the reference to the "end" which is crucial, as we see in the words of Angelos Philippou: "It is man's destiny to share by grace in all which the Holy Trinity possesses by nature."[12]

The difference between West and East is, then, the difference between the *theologia crucis* and the *theologia gloriae.* In the East the self is defined personally and relationally, as is the Trinity. The definition of the self is incomplete without reference to divinity, just as the definition of the deity is incomplete without reference to humanity. The doctrine of the incarnation is as much a statement about humanity as it is about divinity. Zizioulas faithfully represents Eastern theology when he traces the general Western notion of personhood to the Orthodox interpretation of the Trinity. "To be" is "to be in relation"; "Being is Communion."

III. THE RELATIONAL SELF

The True Self Is the Relational Self

The true self is to be understood relationally, that is, in terms of a relational metaphysics according to which only relation, relating, is real.[13] This assumption entails the further step that the terms of a relation, the *relata*, are derivatives. The subject and object of a relation are co-derivatives, in that they emerge coordinately by the same operation. It follows from this that reality consists of experienc*ing;* the experienc*er* and the experienc*ed* (*other*) are co-derivatives of the experienc*ing.*

To the extent that we speak of this experienc*ing* in dualities, we run the risk of replacing reality with abstractions. To the extent that we reify these abstractions, we fall victim to what Whitehead called "the fallacy of misplaced concreteness." Subjects and objects are such a duality, which, when invested with specificity, become candidates for reification. It is different with "I-Thou," since those who favored this expression, such as Feuerbach and Buber, did not intend for it to be taken as a duality. Despite the title of Buber's book on the subject, he gives no meaning to the expression "I *and* Thou." To the contrary, the key to "I-Thou" lies in the hyphen, in what Buber called "the Between." The expression "I-It" functions differently, in that it stands for "I *and* It." It follows that "I-Thou" converts into "Self-Other," and "I-It" into "Subject-Self and Object-Other." While the latter pair of terms exhibits abstract co-derivatives, "Self-Other" is not a duality. Probably the most important claim made by Buber is "the I of I-Thou is different from the I of I-It." Whereas the "I" of "I-It" can be separated from the "It," the "I" of "I-Thou" is — to use the words of Feuerbach to whom in this regard Buber is admittedly indebted — "only a linguistic ellipse that, merely, for brevity's sake, leaves out half of what is understood by itself."[14] This leads to the inevitable next step.

The Relational Self Is the Self of "Self-Other"

There is a grave tendency to think of "other" as "nonmutual," simply because we mean by "other" the "non-I." But the deepest sense of the "other" is "what is mutual." The claim made at the beginning of this essay, "There is no-self, and it is the relational self," now becomes clearer. Preserving the term *self* in the expression "the relational self" respects the fact that in every experienc*ing* there is what Heidegger called "Jemeinigkeit" ("mineness"). This "mineness" is neither a subject nor an ego. Heidegger tried to exhibit due sensitivity to this insight by speaking of the "self" as *Dasein.*

What then is the meaning of "self-other"? It must be that in experienc*ing,* the "self" is defined by the relat*ing,* just as is the "other." Thus it follows that the "self" of "self-other" is not the agent of the experiencing, nor is the "other" of "self-other" the patient. Accordingly, the relational self is "no-self."

The Relational Self Is the Self of Pure Experience

One of the clearest statements on pure experience appeared in Nishida Kitaro's first book, *An Inquiry into the Good*, first published in 1911. The words are memorable:

> To experience means to know facts just as they are, to know in accordance with facts by completely relinquishing one's own fabrications. What we usually refer to as experience is adulterated with some sort of thought, so by *pure* I am referring to the state of experience just as it is without the least addition of deliberative discrimination. The moment of seeing a color or hearing a sound, for example, is prior not only to the thought that the color or sound is the activity of an external object or that one is sensing it, but also to the judgment of what color or sound might be. In this regard, pure experience is identical with direct experience. When one directly experiences one's own state of consciousness, there is not yet a subject or an object, and knowing and its object are completely unified. This is the most refined type of experience.[15]

On this view there is no ego or agent self which precedes and initiates its acts; there is only the act*ing*. It follows that in pure experience there is no prior or posterior, no inner and outer, no will preceding act. All is a unity. It is only from reflection that these components arise. They are but abstractions derivative from experience, formed in accordance with the questions asked about the experience.

One of Nishida's close associates, Nishitani Keiji, has restated the former's meaning as follows:

> To speak of a mind that sees things, a self within that views what is on the outside, does not refer to experience in its pure form but only in a later explanation of experience. In direct experience there is no self, no thing, nothing separate or in-

dividual at all. There is only a bond of many things into a single living whole. This is the way it is with what we call the universe or the world.[16]

Claiming that "there is a single life that vitalizes the universe as a whole," he continues:

In reality no separate individual things exist on their own. Nor is there any separate, individual self. The only such self is the one we have thought up; nothing in reality is so patterned. What exists in reality is at one with the Life of the universe. This view may seem to leave us out of the picture altogether, but it only means that in our looking and listening the activities of looking and listening have emerged somewhere from the depths of the universe. Our looking and listening and all other things we do issue from a point where all things form a single living bond. This is why these activities are united with all sorts of other things and why we cannot think in terms of things existing on the outside and a mind existing on the inside. This is a later standpoint; the prior standpoint is that of pure experience where subject and object are one and undifferentiated.[17]

To distinguish Nishida's notion from that of "immediate experience" in the thought of psychologists like James, Nishitani argues for a "true pure experience."[18]

In pure experience there is no-self and this no-self is the relational self. It is only reflection upon it which generates (i.e., co-dependently originates) a subjective and objective aspect. There is great wisdom in Nishida's view that "it is not that there is experience because there are individuals, but rather there are individuals because of experience."[19] Nishida would probably have regarded even the notion of "mineness" as potentially "impure," and justifiably so because of the tendency we have of reifying all such distinctions. Even Nishitani admits that Nishida's notion of pure experience in An Inquiry into the Good was "entirely subjective," yet he hastens to note that it does not entail the "dichotomy of subject and object or of mind and matter."[20] The equivalent to Heidegger's notion of "mineness" in Nishida's thesis of pure experience is to be found in his claim that — to use Nishitani's words again—"I am myself present in what is going on . . . the scene and my own presence there are the same thing."[21]

The question naturally arises as to the status of the "other" in Nishida's notion of pure experience. His view, as restated by Nishitani, is consistent with the thesis stated above that the relational self is the self of "Self-Other"; "Here 'self-' indicates something that is at once different from an 'other' (and not only an 'other person') and at the same time something of which it can be said 'self and other are neither one nor two.' In other words, it is unity that is neither simply discriminated from every sort of other nor simply not discriminated from it."[22] This view could be restated in perichoretic terms as follows: the "self" and "other" in the formula "self-other" are distinct but not separate.

Only No-Self Is Relational

I have argued elsewhere[23] that the self is its relations; that a change in its relations would mean a change in its character; and that it dissolves with the dissolution of all its relations. It follows from these assumptions that the relational self is not something in itself, some essential or substantial nature which possesses properties. Rather, it is neither more nor less than those properties themselves—properties that represent its relations. Altering David Bohm's words relative to the status of "things" in the Copenhagen Theory,[24] we could say that no self has its own intrinsic properties belonging to itself alone; rather, it shares its properties with all other selves/things. Nishida's notion of the "personal" as a "focus" of the "self-expression of the world" has affinities with this "field theory" of the self, as we may call it. Nishitani's interpretation of Nishida's notion reads as follows:

> Each of us is one of the focal points for the world's creative self-awareness. In giving birth to an infinite number of such focal points of self-awareness, the world reflects itself in them and becomes creative in the process. We do not of course reflect the world by standing outside the world, independent of it. To say that we reflect the world means that we exist as self-conscious beings, that we live and act. This is not to deny ourselves independence. That we exist as self-conscious indi-

viduals independent of one another and that we live and act as such, *is* the world's reflection of itself in us as its foci of self-awareness. We are what Leibniz called "living mirrors of the universe."[25]

The Relational Self Is the Religious Self

For Eckhart, the Orthodox, Buber, and Nishida the "true self" is a spiritual reality. What may be less well known is the way in which Nishida uses the language of theism to express the heart of his vision of selfhood. Accepting the Western view that "the general definition of religion" is "a relationship between God and the human person,"[26] Nishida speaks of God as "the foundation of the universe"— but he maintains that the universe is "not something created by God but an expression or manifestation of the divine."[27] In speaking of the relation of God to the self he appeals to the notion of "divine-human identity,"[28] and even of "the divine-human union."[29] Nishitani at one point summarizes Nishida's position on the self as follows: "To know the true self is to become one with God."[30]

The resonance of this language from the founder of the "Kyoto School" with that of Eckhart, Orthodox theology, and Buber is apparent. In the traditions of Judaism, Christianity, and Zen their visions of selfhood are represented in proprietary symbols and notions with the result that the parallels between them have often been overlooked or are — at worst — vigorously denied. My intention in this essay has been to focus on an insight into selfhood which transcends their parochial boundaries.

NOTES

1. Krister Stendahl, *Paul among Jews and Gentiles and Other Essays* (Philadephia: Fortress Press, 1976), pp. 78–96; first published in the *Harvard Theological Review* 56 (1963): 199–215.

2. Michael Theunissen, *The Other: Studies in the Social Ontology of Husserl, Heidegger, Sartre and Buber*, trans. Christopher Macann (Cambridge, Mass.: Massachusetts Institute of Technology Press, 1984).

3. Robert N. Bellah, Richard Madsen, William M. Sullivan, Ann

Swidler, and Steven M. Tipton, *Habits of the Heart: Individualism and Commitment in American Life* (Berkeley: University of California Press, 1985), p. viii.

4. Cited from "Wisdom in Emptiness: A Dialogue by Daisetz T. Suzuki and Thomas Merton," in *Zen and the Birds of Appetite* by Thomas Merton (New York: New Directions, 1968), p. 109.

5. Robert B. Blakney, ed., *Meister Eckhart: A Modern Translation* (New York: Harper & Row, Modern Torchbook, 1941), p. 288.

6. This theme is developed in more detail in my essay "Western Introspection and the Temporalizing of the Will," in Harold H. Oliver, *Relatedness: Essays in Metaphysics and Theology* (Macon, Ga.: Mercer University Press, 1984), pp. 65–78.

7. Baron von Hügel, "St. John, Gospel of," *Encyclopedia Britannica*, 11th ed. (Cambridge: At the University Press, 1911), vol. 15, p. 454.

8. Blakney, *Meister Eckhart*, p. 212.

9. John D. Zizioulas, *Being as Communion: Studies in Personhood and the Church* (Crestwood, N.Y.: St. Vladimir's Seminary Press, 1985).

10. Angelos J. Philippou, "The Mystery of Pentecost," in *The Orthodox Ethos: Essays in Honor of the Centenary of the Greek Orthodox Archdiocese of North and South America*, ed. Angelos J. Philippou (Oxford: Holywell Press, 1964), p. 91.

11. Nikos A. Nissiotis, "The Importance of the Doctrine of the Trinity for Church Life and Theology," in Philippou, *The Orthodox Ethos*, p. 60.

12. Philippou, "The Mystery of the Pentecost," p. 91.

13. For my presentation and defense of relational metaphysics, see Harold H. Oliver, *A Relational Metaphysic: Studies in Philosophy and Religion 4* (The Hague: Martinus Nijhoff Pubs., 1981), and *Relatedness*.

14. Ludwig Feuerbach, "Über Spiritualismus und Materialismus, besonders in Beziehung auf die Willensfreiheit," in *Gesammelte Werke*, ed. Werner Schuffenhauer (Berlin: Akademische Verlag, 1972), vol. 11: *Kleinere Schriften* 4 (1851–1866), par. 15.

15. Kitaro Nishida, *An Inquiry into the Good*, trans. Masao Abe and Christopher Ives (New Haven: Yale University Press, 1990), pp. 1f.

16. Nishitani Keiji, *Nishida Kitaro*, trans. Yamamoto Seisaku and James Heisig (Berkeley: University of California Press, 1991), p. 54.

17. Ibid., pp. 54–55.

18. Ibid., p. 81.

19. Ibid., p. 148.

20. Ibid., pp. 33f.

21. Ibid., p. 96.

22. Ibid., pp. 105f.

23. Oliver, *A Relational Metaphysic,* and *Relatedness.*

24. David Bohm, *Causality and Chance in Modern Physics* (London: Routledge & Kegan Paul, 1957), p. 147.

25. Nishitani, *Nishida Kitaro,* p. 36.

26. Ibid., p. 148.

27. Cited in Nishitani, *Nishida Kitaro,* pp. 148f.

28. Ibid., pp. 174, 177.

29. Ibid.

30. Ibid., p. 147.

Limits of the Social and Rational Self

LAWRENCE E. CAHOONE

IN A MEMORABLE SCENE in James Clavell's *Shogun* a group of ship-wrecked English sailors are imprisoned in a pit in early seventeenth-century Japan. Told by their captors that they must select one of their group to be killed, the ten men draw straws. When the samurai come to take the selected man a fight erupts, with the result that another man is dragged away in his place. At sundown he is trussed like a chicken, placed in a large cauldron, head exposed, and slowly boiled. It takes him until dawn to die. During the night, the local feudal lord, who has ordered this torture, meditates on the screams.[1]

Let us do the same, but for a different purpose. Suppose that we are among the men in the pit during the night. We hear the screams. We can imagine, in some sense, not only the pain but the utter helplessness of the victim, surrounded by aliens who regard him as an animal to be used in any way desired, unconstrained by moral limits. What is happening to him is the worst thing that can happen to a human being, utter calamity.

Among the many thoughts that might occur to us in the pit, two are of interest here. The first is, "It could have been me." Any one of us might have been selected. For the purposes of the torturers, we are more or less equivalent. Relative to being subjected to the worst calamity that any of us can imagine, there is no significant difference between ourselves and the man in the pot. Connected with this thought is an empathy, a virtual sharing of the pain and terror of the victim. *It could have been me.* During the long night in the pit, we meditate on our comrade's screams, which are very close to being our screams.

The second thought, which we must imagine eventually to follow the terror of the first, is: "But it wasn't me!" For the fact

53

is that we are not in the cauldron; he is. And this difference is the most important difference in the world to us. It outweighs all other facts; it is an absolute difference. Whether we respond to this thought with happy indifference to his suffering or deep sorrow or even guilt, it remains that nothing else is as significant to our lives as the fact that we are here and he is there, that *it wasn't me.*

This gruesome tale serves as an illustration of an obvious fact, that while in many respects we are the same and so share a common predicament, we remain separate individuals. One of the many philosophical implications of this fact is that any perspective on human being that describes us in terms of what is shared among us, of our being members of a community or instances of a rule, cannot exhaust all that is true about us. There is, for all such perspectives, something left out, an *asocial* remainder, as it were. The singularity of each self, the fact of its separateness, is irreducible.

Recent developments in diverse areas of philosophical research have unintentionally supplied a context in which this irreducible singularity takes on an unexpected significance. If rationality is inherently social — as a number of philosophers have suggested — then the asocial is nonrational. And if we are irreducibly asocial, then we are irreducibly irrational too.[2]

I

Recent years have witnessed a shift in American philosophical attention towards the communal or social nature of human being. This *neosocialism,* which need not have anything to do with political economy, has perhaps been meant to counteract the cumulative pressure of earlier forms of individualism — political, ethical, epistemic, and semantic — held to be characteristic of liberalism, capitalism, Cartesianism, and modernism. Talk of such a turn across widely divergent areas of philosophy must, of course, remain impressionistic. But there seems to be resurging recognition of the communal nature of human being and human cognition sweeping across different philosophical concerns.

Wittgenstein's *Philosophical Investigations* was famous for its attack on the possibility of private languages, making semantics public and social; its influence in this regard has been vast.[3] Since Thomas Kuhn's *The Structure of Scientific Revolutions* (1962), the philosophy of science has witnessed growing attention to the sociology and social history of knowledge.[4] There has been a renewed interest in classical American pragmatism, sparked in particular by Hilary Putnam and Richard Rorty.[5] In particular, the founder of pragmatism, Charles Sanders Peirce, has begun to receive appreciative attention. Peirce, John Dewey, George Herbert Mead, and Josiah Royce all emphasized the social nature of the human individual. Peirce defined truth and logic in terms of community, a point to which we will return.

In ethics and political theory, there has been a renewed interest in Hegel, Aquinas, and Aristotle, in response to the egocentric, associational, or "nominalistic" liberalism allegedly characteristic of the North Atlantic political culture of the nineteenth and twentieth centuries.[6] This move is evident in the work of Michael Sandel, Alasdair MacIntyre, and Charles Taylor, to name but a few.[7] The communitarianism of Robert Bellah, the traditionalism of Edward Shils and Alan Bloom, and the thesis of the demise of the public sphere offered earlier by Hannah Arendt and more recently by Richard Sennett are further evidence of this neosocialism.[8]

Despite political differences with Neo-Aristotelianism, Neo-Hegelianism, and communitarianism, the work of Karl-Otto Apel and Jürgen Habermas exhibits the same social turn. Habermas's critique of late modern society and his suggested foundation for ethics are based on Apel's notion that the most basic form of rationality is fundamentally "communicative" or interpersonal.[9] It is no accident that Apel and Habermas are two of the very few European philosophers who draw on the American pragmatists: Apel on Peirce, and Habermas, most importantly, on Mead.

A point of intersection between these semantic and epistemic developments on the one hand and the ethical and political work on the other is the notion of rationality. This is the heart of the whole movement: there is a growing tendency to interpret rationality as a social or communal phenomenon. This does not necessarily imply conventionalism, or the view that what is rational is the product of agreement. Ignoring the many variations among its proponents, the minimal commitment of current neosocialism is that rationality is an *interpersonal* and *public* phenomenon. This claim is often promoted in opposition to the effects of a Cartesian tradition that made rationality the trait of individuals, capable of exercise even with the existence of the social world in doubt.

For example, in his monumental *The Theory of Communicative Action* (1981; English translation, 1984 and 1987), Habermas presented an account of "communicative rationality" to counteract the "instrumental" conception of rationality dominant in modern social theory. Instrumental rationality remains "subjective" in the sense that it serves personal aims. Communicative rationality, on the other hand, is intrinsically interpersonal; it is an attempt to justify one's claims or actions through recourse to reasons acceptable to others. It is communication "oriented to achieving understanding" or consensus. Democracy is nothing other than that political system in which this kind of communication has achieved a decisive role in determining the course of social action.

According to Habermas, not only did the theorists of society, like Max Weber, fail to take communicative rationality sufficiently into account, and so — upon recognizing the subjectivism of instrumental reason — fall into subjectivism or irrationalism. The very development of modern society has exhibited the disintegration of communicative reason in favor of the instrumental rationality characteristic of the money- and power-driven, bureaucratic-economic "system." The reinvigoration of the modern democracies will require that communicative rationality gain control over the system.

Habermas draws on the congenial view of Mead, who analyzed rationality in terms of the ability to take up the perspective of others.[10] "Man," for Mead, "is a rational being because he is a social being."[11] This has consequences for ethics, for "those ends are good which lead to the realization of the self as a social being."[12] Following Apel, Habermas attempts to answer ethical skepticism in the pragmatic spirit by drawing ethical principles from the necessary presuppositions of rational communication, creating a theory of "discourse ethics."

From a different perspective, in his two volumes, *After Virtue* (1981) and *Whose Justice? Which Rationality?* (1988), Alasdair MacIntyre presented a critique of what he regards as the dominant ideology of Western modernity, liberalism.[13] Liberalism misunderstands the nature of rationality, and thus of human being, as universal, ahistorical, and culture-independent. MacIntyre retorts that "man without culture is a myth."[14] Rationality must be defined in terms of progressive problem solving within an "enquiry-bearing" tradition; there is no rationality *per se*, only rationality-in-a-tradition. Such traditions are not monolithic; they are ongoing conversations among related but divergent viewpoints addressing deep issues. MacIntyre recommends that we recognize the tradition-embeddedness of rationality, and the need to return to the notion of an intrinsic human *telos* as providing the framework for moral reasoning, as in the Aristotelian and Thomist traditions.

These impulses are shared by communitarians and other critics of the liberal individualist tradition. But the Kantian ethical tradition, evident in the liberalism of John Rawls and Habermas, accepts the primacy of the socialized self as thoroughly as does communitarianism. Certainly there are differences. For Kantians, ethical rationality presumes identification with an imagined or possible community — whether "the kindom of ends" in Kant, the "initial position" in Rawls, or Habermas's principles "U" (universalization) and "D" (discourse).[15] The Hegelian community, in contrast, is an actual, particular, historical community. The possible community is imagined along universalist lines, in which I am one among a number of equal and functionally indistinguishable persons; whereas in the actual community, my identity may be linked to a particular role.[16]

However, for the Kantian, Hegelian, and Aristotelian traditions, for Habermas and MacIntyre, for Rawls and Sandel, what is relevant to rationality, therefore to the moral good, is the identification of the individual with others. It is that perspective for which *I am no different from others* that is crucial to rationality in its epistemic and practical employments. This holds even if the community assigns me a special role in a community of hierarchical differences. For that role is never unique to me: it is historically determined, was occupied by my predecessor and will be occupied by my successor. Its current occupant belongs to the community, and to the duties of his or her role; the role does not belong to the occupant. Whether my sameness is determined by actual membership in such an historical community or by imaginative identification with an ideal community, whether it is differentially modulated by a role in a hierarchical structure or determined by the abstract equality among instances of a universal rule — in either case, it is by identifying the self with present, past, and possible others, and thereby disregarding my uniqueness, that I am rational.

Charles S. Peirce, inventor of pragmatism and a dozen other doctrines, was famous for his socialized view of reason. He believed this socialization was entirely compatible with a realist view of knowledge and its objects. Since so much of neosocialism exhibits the influence of pragmatism, it is important to understand Peirce's views in some detail.

Peirce defines truth as that opinion on which the community of inquirers is destined to converge in the long run. Reality is the object of that true opinion. Hence,

> the very origin of the conception of reality shows that this conception essentially involves the notion of a COMMUNITY, without definite limits, and capable of a definite increase of knowledge.[17]

A particularly important text in regard to Peirce's view of rationality is his remarkable 1868 essay, "Grounds of Validity of the Laws of Logic." It constitutes Peirce's attempt to answer skepticism, in particular, Hume's skeptical attack on the validity of induction. How is it that, given present experience of part of a class of things, we can know something about future experience of the rest of the class? This is Hume's problem of induction, to which Kant answered with the invention of transcendental philosophy.

Peirce gave this question great importance. Whereas Kant asked, how are synthetic *a priori* judgments possible, Peirce remarks,

> But antecedently to this comes the question how synthetical judgments in general, and still more generally, how synthetical reasoning is possible at all. . . . This is the lock on the door of philosophy.[18]

The validity of probable inference, for example, the inference from the proportion of black and white beans in a sample to the proportion in the collection from which the sample was drawn, rests on one fact: "in the long run, any one bean would be taken out as often as any other,"[19] or any one bean will as often appear in the sample, hence in the premise of the induction. But the real character of the collection is, according to Peirce's definition of reality, reflected in the judgment about the collection which holds true in the long run. Hence Peirce justifies induction by his convergence theory of reality. His explanation is one of the most convincing presentations of that theory (despite its final, unappealing metaphor).

> Upon our theory of reality and of logic, it can be shown that no inference of any individual can be thoroughly logical without certain determinations of his mind which do not concern any one inference immediately; for we have seen that that mode of inference which alone can teach us anything, or carry us at all beyond what was implied in our premises — in fact, does not give us to know any more than we knew before; only, we know that, by faithfully adhering to that mode of inference, we shall, on the whole, approximate to the truth. Each of us is an insurance company, in short.[20]

It is the continuous or general nature of inference and of reality that explains and validates induction. No one inference is valid. For Peirce, "the validity of induction depends simply upon the fact that the parts make up . . . the whole."[21]

This leads to an interesting claim. For, given that validity is in the collection of inferences, if someone has a "transcendent personal interest" that outweighs all others, Peirce says, he or she "can make no valid inference whatever." In other words,

> logic rigidly requires, before all else, that no determinate fact, nothing which can happen to a man's self, should be of more consequence to him than everything else.[22]

The individual thinker and the individual datum cannot outweigh the many. The "ideal perfection of knowledge," which "constitutes" reality for Peirce, presumes complete identification of each individual with the interests of an indefinite or possible community.[23] Logic is thought identified with the whole. Absent the appropriation of the term by political economy, Peirce's theory ought to be called a socialist theory of logic.[24]

Ten years later, Peirce published a series of essays, "Illustrations of the Logic of Science," in which he set out the doctrine of pragmatism.[25] One of the essays in the series, "The Doctrine of Chances," explicates his social theory of logic with an intriguing example. Imagine someone faced with the following choice. There are two packs of cards, one containing twenty-five black cards and one red card, and another containing twenty-five red cards and one black card. One card must be picked from one of the two packs. If a red card is drawn, "eternal felicity" will be his or her fate; if a black card, "everlasting woe." This is a more complex case of the sailors in the pit, drawing straws.

According to Peirce's analysis of probable reasoning, neither choice is rational, since the case is unrepeatable. Probability presumes a series of inferences; "in reference to a single case considered in itself, probability can have no meaning."[26] For a probable inference—"if A, then B"—to be true, there must be some "real fact" such that "*whenever* such an event as A happens such an event as B happens," a fact to which the inference corresponds. But there is no such real fact in this case: there is no "whenever," because the case is unrepeatable. As Hilary Putnam remarks on Peirce's example, "A person can have eternal felicity or everlasting woe only once!"[27]

The problem is, Peirce admits, that with respect to our imagined subject, "it would be folly to deny that he ought to prefer the pack containing the larger proportion of red cards."[28] In other words, we would all insist on choosing a card from that pack, despite its apparent irrationality. How to account for our choice?

Peirce pushes the problem further. The same predicament holds regarding all the choices or "chances" of a person's life if we take them collectively as one unrepeatable choice. Not only is our success in life—the attainment of more satisfactions than disappointments over a lifetime—uncertain; it is worse than that. Peirce claims,

> It is an indubitable result of the theory of probabilities that every gambler, if he continues long enough, must ultimately be ruined.[29]

For, given finite resources, eventually the gambler must lose enough that he or she does not have sufficient remaining resources to win back everything (actually, everything plus one dollar) on the next bet. "The same thing is true," Peirce says, "of an insurance company," whose losses must eventually ruin it. The gamble that constitutes human life must end in loss. Peirce writes,

> All human affairs rest upon probabilities, and the same thing is true everywhere. If man were immortal he could be perfectly sure of seeing the day when everything in which he had trusted should betray his trust, and, in short, of coming eventually to hopeless misery. He would break down, at last, as every great fortune, as every dynasty, as every civilization does. In place of this we have death.[30]

That is, for individuals death limits the series of bets, and so makes it uncertain whether we will go out as losers.

How, then, to explain our selection of the mostly red pack, despite the fact that the choice cannot be repeated? The only explanation, Peirce says, is that we *must* identify "our interests with those of an unlimited community."

> It seems to me that we are driven to this, that logicality inexorably requires that our interests shall *not* be limited. They must not stop at our own fact, but must embrace the whole community. This community, again, must not be limited, but must extend to all races of beings with whom we can come into immediate or mediate intellectual relation. It must reach, however vaguely, beyond this geological epoch, beyond all bounds. *He who would not sacrifice his own soul to save the whole world, is, as it seems to me, illogical in all his inferences, collectively.* Logic is rooted in the social principle.[31]

Peirce admits in both essays that there is no evidence whatsoever for the assumption that the community will "ever arrive at a state of information greater than some definite finite information,"[32] or that the human community "will exist forever."[33] There is not a "scintilla" of evidence to show that intelligent life will exist at any future moment. But neither is there any evidence against it.[34] Hence, our belief in the indefinitely extensive and enduring community is a necessary "hope," in the Kantian spirit. In "Grounds of Validity of the Laws of Logic," Peirce says of the assumption of the possible perfection or completion of knowledge, that it

> involves a transcendent and supreme interest, and therefore from its very nature is unsusceptible of any support from reasons. This infinite hope which we all have . . . is something so august and momentous, *that all reasoning in reference to it is a trifling impertinence.* We do not want to know what are the weights of reasons *pro* and *con* — that is, how much *odds* we should wish to receive on such a venture in the long run — because there is no long run in the case; the question is single and supreme, and ALL is at stake upon it.[35]

The belief in the in-principle inevitability of the completion of knowledge is a necessary presupposition we must make, and it cannot be justified by reasons and evidence. That is, it is an issue whose valid resolution *cannot be imagined via the notion of the long run,* and hence, *via the notion of the indefinitely extended community.* It is an issue that stands *outside* the series of inferences, the progress of inquiry, since it concerns a *condition of* that series and its progress. Peirce seems close to founding reason on an irrational leap of faith. But, he immediately continues,

> we are in the condition of a man in a life and death struggle; if he have not sufficient strength, it is wholly indifferent to him how he acts, so that the only assumption upon which he can act rationally is the hope of success. So this sentiment is rigidly demanded by logic . . . it is always a hypothesis . . . justified by its indispensableness for making any action rational.[36]

In this remarkable passage, Peirce seeks to close the circle, to make the choice to be rational — a choice that must take place outside the realm of evidence — *a rational choice,* indeed, a "rigidly" logical one. At this point his imagery has shifted to the practical and the naturalistic. The justification for the logical nature of the choice to be logical is the instrumental value of rational action, which increases our chances of success in the "life and death struggle." Yet Peirce emphasizes elsewhere that rationality, and especially rational inquiry, is impractical and much inferior to instinct and sentiment as a guide in life. Regarding "vital" matters, reason is no help at all. Even on Peircean grounds, the hypothesis that logical method will bring success is not our only option.[37]

II

That the self's identification with others is necessary and virtually universal cannot reasonably be denied. Every human being living a human life must identify with others. To fail to do so would be catastrophic for the individual. For example, it would make language learning and social relationships impossible. However, this is not to say that the identification with others exhausts the self, that the self judges *everything* from a socialized standpoint. The dimension in which there is no significant difference between oneself and others does not exhaust what is significant about the self, and hence, does not exhaust the perspectives from which the self's judgments are made. This means that the self can and sometimes does judge the world from the point of view of the singularity and difference of the self, not the sameness of the self. For such "asocial" perspectives, the difference between oneself and others is the most important fact of all.

We might imagine that most selves most of the time make judgments on the basis of some combination of social and asocial perspectives. We might further imagine that the relative weight of these two kinds of perspectives varies, and that it is only for very rare persons, or in very rare moments, that the social perspective is rendered negligible. Certain experiences do highlight what is not shared, what is singular, making the difference between oneself and others paramount, bringing the asocial to the foreground and relegating the social to the background. Calamity, the greatest being death, often exhibits this with arresting clarity.

This rather simple fact of our singularity is reflected in some not-so-simple philosophical issues, for example, in the problem of "egoism" in ethics. In *A Theory of Justice* John Rawls ruled out egoism as a possible ethical position on formal grounds. And he is certainly right that egoism cannot supply an ethical principle, since ethical principles cannot be based on the singularity of oneself. But this does not in itself constitute a reason to *give up* egoism. It can only count as a reason against egoism for someone who is not an egoist, that is, someone who already identifies with others and hence accepts the need for a generalizable ethical principle.

Trying to convince someone not to be an egoist is like trying to give someone reasons to be moral, or reasons to be rational. In the terms of our concerns here, that problem becomes one of giving reasons why someone ought to identify with others. Only someone who already identifies with others would find such reasons compelling. At this level, we always preach to the converted. Of course, we can cite non-normative causes, as opposed to reasons, to the unconverted, like, "If you fail to identify with others we will cook you." In other words, we can compel such people with force, but we cannot compel them with norms.

I propose to accept the neosocialist turn in defining rationality. I accept that the best account of rationality we currently have identifies it in some sense with sociality. Again, this is not to make rationality a product of social convention, but rather a quality or function of human interaction. This social theory of rationality has an unforeseen consequence, however. If we accept it, then we must allow that when a human being makes judgments from an asocial perspective — a perspective for which the difference between oneself and others is absolute — we cannot describe the judgments made as rational. That is, we must admit that there are nonrational judgments and nonrational perspectives.

This conclusion may seem tame enough. In this post-Freudian century we are accustomed to talk of an irrational dimension of the self. The present suggestion is, however, not without its special implications. The social concept of rationality opposes the rational not to the passionate or the instinctive, but to the unique or asocial. It is an unavoidable fact that we are singular and unique. My claim is that whenever that fact becomes the most important fact in determining our judgments, those judgments fail to be rational in light of the social theory of rationality.

One qualification is that persons can identify with others in regard to some matters and not others. The most radical example is the psychopath. We cannot say that the psychopath fails to take up the perspective of others totally or simply. For such a failure would make social living quite impossible in a practical sense. The psychopath can be, as we know, expert at playing all sorts of social games. But he or she does not identify with, or take the perspective of, others in crucial respects. Identification with society is fully adequate up to a point, at which it disappears entirely. The psychopath's daily public behavior, for example, is likely to be quite socialized, while his or her judgment about the value of the life of a stranger may be utterly unsocialized.

III

I have suggested that the self is incompletely social in its identifications, hence incompletely rational. My further, less modest hypothesis is that the two perspectives are *not rationally reconcilable.* The choice as to whether to view phenomena from the social or asocial perspectives, in the former of which my differences from others are negligible and in the latter of which they are absolute, cannot be a rational one. It is ir- or non-rational because rationality does — as the neosocialist turn has it — appear to be an artifact of social identification. There can be, therefore, no rational choice to identify with others, just as there could be no rational choice to be rational.

Within the orbit of the history of philosophy, the effect of this claim is to move away from the related paths of Aristotle, Kant, Hegel, and the American pragmatists, and to declare an allegiance with existentialism in general and with Kierkegaard in particular. It is in Kierkegaard's rebellion against Hegel that we find the most articulate denial of the possibility of a reconciliation of the social or rational and the individual.

In *Fear and Trembling*, Kierkegaard identifies the ethical and the social with the universal.[38] The ethical or universal viewpoint, for which nothing is "incommensurable," idiosyncratic, irreconcilable, or hidden, has no room for the uniquely personal. In the "ethical view of life," the individual is required to "strip himself" of whatever is idiosyncratic or hidden, that is, of his or her "interiority."[39] He writes,

> The ethical as such is the universal; as the universal it is in turn the disclosed. The single individual, qualified as immediate, sensate, and psychical, is the hidden. Thus his ethical task is to work himself out of his hiddenness and to become disclosed in the universal.[40]

Faith transcends and contradicts the ethical and the social. Kierkegaard explains his point by means of the tale of Abraham and Isaac. God told Abraham to take his beloved son up to the mountain and sacrifice him. Abraham had drawn the knife and was about to strike when God stopped him. God's command had been a test; Isaac would be spared. Abraham sacrificed a ram instead.

The aim of Kierkegaard's reading of this story is to drive home the opposition of the religious and the ethical. The ethical law is not to kill, and to kill one's child is the greatest abomination in human society. God's command, and Abraham's obedience, are unethical. In his faith, Abraham abrogates the ethical obligation of a father to his son and cements an "absolute" relation to God. This relation is private and unique; it admits no social constraints and literally cannot be understood. It is not rational: "Faith is this paradox, and the single individual simply cannot make himself understandable to anyone."[41]

Now, as we know, faith for Kierkegaard is absurd. The "knight of faith" renounces his love, for example, but says to himself, "Nevertheless I have faith that I will get her—that is, by virtue of the absurd, by virtue of the fact that for God all things are possible."[42] The knight "acknowledges the impossibility, and in the very same moment he believes the absurd. . . ."[43] If what is believed is not absurd, not literally a rational impossibility, then belief in it cannot be faith.

Faith violates the ethical, and hence, the rational, the universal, the social.

> For if the ethical—that is, social morality—is the highest and if there is in a person no residual incommensurability in some way such that this incommensurability is not evil . . . then no categories are needed other than what Greek philosophy had. . . . [44]

In other words, if ethics is the highest human possibility, then social categories are sufficient and faith is irrelevant. Where there is faith, it is "this paradox that the single individual is higher than the universal." Differently put, faith is a "teleological suspension of the ethical."

The opposition of the ethical and the religious, or the paradoxical situation of faith, cannot be reconciled. Kierkegaard insists that

> the single individual as the single individual stands in an absolute relation to the absolute. This position cannot be mediated, for *all mediation takes place only by virtue of the universal*, it is and remains for all eternity a paradox, impervious to thought.[45]

My current suggestion is that Kierkegaard is right that the choice between identification with the community and the perspective for which the difference between oneself and others is absolute cannot be a rational one. In so far as it is a choice at all, the choice as to whether or not to identify with the community must be a *criterion-less* choice, a choice without a reason. It may, of course, have a cause; something may compel the choice. Reasons are not what is compelling, but what *ought* to be compelling. There can be no *ought* in this case.

Let us illustrate the point with one last tale, this time a true one. In late July 1945, after completing an urgent and secret mission that took it to the Southwest Pacific island of Tinian, the USS *Indianapolis* with its twelve hundred men was struck by Japanese torpedoes in the middle of the Pacific night. It sank within fifteen minutes. The eight hundred men who survived the sinking went into the water, strung over twenty miles of ocean because the ship had continued forward until it sank. The great majority were without life rafts, supported by life vests or belts. The sharks appeared within a few hours. No search was initiated. After four days in the water, they were accidentally spotted from the air, and 320 were picked up. Only then did they learn what their mission had been: they had delivered the atom bomb to Tinian, from which the *Enola Gay* had flown to immolate Hiroshima.

During four days in the water, all manner of human traits arose: heroism, murder, sexuality, paranoia, suicide, determination to survive. Death came randomly from below.

> When a shark approached a group, everyone would kick, punch, and create a general racket. This often worked, and the predator would leave. At other times, however, the shark "would have singled out his victim and no amount of shouts or pounding of the water would turn him away. . . ."[46]

Some hoarded food, even resorting to violence. After three days in the water, many were delirious and paranoid. Many of the men "wanted to be alone, for no one trusted anyone else."[47] The ship's doctor recounted how, when drifting by himself, "a man floated by, and [we] instinctively backed away from each other." Even at the risk of dying, many men feared community.

This chaos makes the acts of heroism even more remarkable. Men in lifeboats and with life jackets chose to dive into the water, or to give up their life jackets, to save others. Why, when exhaustion made every expenditure of strength life-threatening, when a drowning man was likely to die later anyway, when others did nothing, did some choose to dive into shark-infested water to save a stranger? How can we characterize the criteria that governed their decision? To cite duty or sympathy is no help, for the question is, why did they so identify with others that duty became relevant and sympathy arose? Why did they choose to see that floating anarchy of desperate men as a community? Why did they act on the thought, "that could be me," rather than, "but it isn't me"?

We have seen that, in so far as their acts were chosen at all, the choice was in effect a choice to make oneself subject to norms, and so could not itself be determined by norms, by an "ought." Like Kierkegaard's faith, it was irrational, although not in the sense of opposing reason, but rather in the sense of not being determined by reason. Of course, that the choice was not normatively determined does not mean it was not determined by causes or motives. But what causes or motives could be strong enough to counteract the obvious motive of survival and the obvious causes of weakness and fear? Here the neosocialist turn may supply more unintended help.

Melville wrote of being abandoned at sea,

> Now, in calm weather, to swim in the open ocean is as easy to the practiced swimmer as to ride in a spring-carriage ashore. But the awful lonesomeness is intolerable. The intense concentration of self in the middle of such a heartless immensity, my God![48]

Likewise, perhaps, is the failure to share the social perspective. The motivation for identifying with others, for imagining community of perspective, may be that to choose the opposite, to choose to be wholly unethical or irrational, is intolerable to us. We could not stand the loneliness. What fascinates and horrifies us in the psychopath may be the self-possession of someone able to live with utter loneliness, something we could not tolerate. And perhaps this is why a man risks his only life to save another, because to fail to do so, to tell himself that "it isn't me," would transport him into an imaginative world too lonely to endure. If morality and rationality are tied to sociality, then it may be that we must be ethical and rational in order to avoid being all alone.

NOTES

1. James Clavell, *Shogun: A Novel of Japan* (New York: Dell, 1975), chap. 4.

2. I will use the terms *nonrational* and *irrational* interchangeably to mean what is not rational. While I will not argue the case here, I accept the implications of my usage, that the irrational or antirational is nothing more than the nonrational. The three terms *rational, nonrational,* and *irrational* do not constitute a triad comparable to, for example, *theism, agnosticism,* and *atheism.*

3. Although Wittgenstein did not invent this approach he gave it a new impetus. See Ludwig Wittgenstein, *Philosophical Investigations,* trans. Elizabeth Anscombe (New York: Macmillan, 1958).

4. See Thomas Kuhn, *The Structure of Scientific Revolutions* (Chicago: University of Chicago Press, 1962).

5. Richard Rorty's most recent efforts can be seen in *Objectivity, Relativism, and Truth* (Cambridge: At the University Press, 1991) and *Essays on Heidegger and Others* (Cambridge: At the University Press, 1991). Hilary Putnam's pragmatism is evident in *Reason, Truth and History* (Cambridge: At the University Press, 1981) and *The Many Faces of Realism* (LaSalle, Ill.: Open Court, 1987), among other works.

6. For the use of the concept of nominalism in this regard, see Eugene Rochberg-Halton, *The Meaning of Modernity* (Chicago: University of Chicago Press, 1986).

7. See Michael Sandel, *Liberalism and the Limits of Justice* (Cambridge: At the University Press, 1982), in which he criticizes John Rawls, *A Theory of Justice* (Cambridge, Mass.: Harvard University Press, 1971). See also Sandel's collection of liberal and antiliberal writings, *Liberalism and Its Critics* (New York: New York University Press, 1984); Alasdair MacIntyre, *After Virtue: A Study in Moral Theory* (Notre Dame, Ind.:

University of Notre Dame Press, 1981) and *Whose Justice? Which Rationality?* (Notre Dame, Ind.: University of Notre Dame Press, 1988); and Charles Taylor, *Sources of the Self: The Making of the Modern Identity* (Cambridge, Mass.: Harvard University Press, 1989).

8. See Robert Bellah et al., *Habits of the Heart: Individualism and Commitment in American Life* (New York: Harper & Row, 1985); Edward Shils, *Tradition* (Chicago: University of Chicago Press, 1981); Alan Bloom, *The Closing of the American Mind* (New York: Simon & Schuster, 1987); Hannah Arendt, *The Human Condition* (Chicago: University of Chicago Press, 1958); and Richard Sennett, *The Fall of Public Man* (New York: Vintage, 1974).

9. See Karl-Otto Apel, "The *A Priori* of the Communication Community and the Foundations of Ethics: The Problem of a Rational Foundation of Ethics in the Scientific Age," in *Towards a Transformation of Philosophy*, trans. Glyn Adey and David Frisby (London: Routledge, 1980) pp. 225–300; and Jürgen Habermas, *The Theory of Communicative Action*, trans. Thomas McCarthy (Boston: Beacon Press, 1981 and 1987), *The Philosophical Discourse of Modernity*, trans. Frederick Lawrence (Cambridge, Mass.: Massachusetts Institute of Technology Press, 1987), and "Discourse Ethics: Notes on a Program of Philosophical Justification," in *Moral Consciousness and Communicative Action*, trans. Christian Lenhardt and Shierry Weber Nicholsen (Cambridge, Mass.: Massachusetts Institute of Technology Press, 1990), pp. 43–115.

10. See George Herbert Mead, *Mind, Self and Society* (Chicago: University of Chicago Press, 1934). Habermas's most extended discussion of Mead is in Habermas, *Theory of Communicative Action*, vol. 2, chap. 5. Habermas also cites Mead in his derivation of the principle of universalization in his "Discourse Ethics," p. 65. Habermas is right to cite Mead here; his principle of universalization is virtually equivalent to Mead's claim that "when it comes to the problem of reconstruction there is one essential demand—that all of the interests that are involved should be taken into account" (Mead, *Mind, Self and Society*, p. 386).

11. Mead, *Mind, Self and Society*, p. 379.

12. Ibid., p. 385.

13. See Alasdair MacIntyre, "Relativism, Power, and Philosophy," a 1985 lecture, reprinted in *After Philosophy: End or Transformation?*, ed. Kenneth Baynes et al. (Cambridge, Mass.: Massachusetts Institute of Technology Press, 1987), pp. 385–411; and *Whose Justice? Which Rationality?* MacIntyre's most recent book is consonant with the relevant points made by these earlier works; see Alasdair MacIntyre, *Three Rival Versions of Moral Enquiry* (Notre Dame, Ind.: University of Notre Dame Press, 1990).

14. MacIntyre, *After Virtue*, p. 161.

15. See Rawls, *Theory of Justice*, chap. 3, and Habermas, "Discourse Ethics."

16. See Peter Berger, "On the Obsolescence of the Concept of Honour," in Sandel, *Liberalism and Its Critics*, pp. 149–58.

17. Charles Sanders Peirce, *Collected Papers*, ed. Charles Hartshorne and Paul Weiss, 8 vols. (Cambridge, Mass.: Harvard University Press, 1931–58), 5.311. (All references are to volume and paragraph number.)

18. Ibid., 5.348.

19. Ibid., 5.349.

20. Ibid., 5.354.

21. Ibid., 5.349.

22. Ibid., 5.354.

23. Ibid., 5.356.

24. The phrase "logical socialism," applied to Peirce, evidently comes from G. Wartenberg, "Logischer Sozialismus" (Ph.D. diss., Frankfurt, 1971). Reference to this work, which I have not seen, is in Apel, *Towards a Transformation of Philosophy*, p. 92.

25. The doctrine was formulated in Peirce, *Collected Papers*, vol. 5: "The Fixation of Belief" (1877) and its sequel, "How To Make Our Ideas Clear" (1878).

26. Peirce, *Collected Papers*, 2.652.

27. Putnam, *Many Faces of Realism*, p. 82. Putnam discusses this Peircean example at some length.

28. Peirce, *Collected Papers*, 2.652.

29. Ibid., 2.653.

30. Ibid.

31. Ibid., 2.654, emphasis added.

32. Ibid., 5.357.

33. Ibid., 2.654.

34. Ibid.

35. Ibid., 5.357, long emphasis added.

36. Ibid.

37. Instinct may be a superior guide. See Peirce, "Vitally Important Topics," in *Collected Papers*, 1.616–77. Also, there are nonscientific methods of fixing belief that have their own virtues. See Peirce, "The Fixation of Belief."

38. Soren Kierkegaard, *Fear and Trembling*, trans. Howard and Edna Hong (Princeton: Princeton University Press, 1983).

39. Ibid., p. 69.

40. Ibid., p. 82.

41. Ibid., p. 71.

42. Ibid., p. 46.

43. Ibid., p. 47.

44. Ibid., p. 55.

45. Ibid., p. 56, emphasis added.

46. Raymond Lech, *All the Drowned Sailors* (New York: Stein & Day, 1982), p. 65.

47. Ibid., p. 85.

48. Herman Melville, *Moby Dick: or, The Whale*, ed. Charles Feidelson, Jr. (Indianapolis: Bobbs-Merrill, 1964), p. 529.

Going Astray:
Weakness, Perversity, or Evil?

EDWARD W. JAMES

To give a philosophical analysis of the self is to make clear that it is both ordinary and extraordinary. The fact that philosophy leaves us with the ordinary self reflects how our lives are untouched by philosophy. While technology, from the horse harness to the computer chip, transforms our lives, philosophy, from Plato to Wittgenstein, leaves everything as it is. Our lives go on no matter what our view of the self is. However, the fact that philosophy unveils the extraordinary self reflects how it is that after a Plato or a Wittgenstein nothing is the same. For to consider the self on philosophical terms is to be astonished by the ordinary. It is to see that what on one level leads us to doze, on another knocks us giddy. For the self as we ordinarily think and live it raises the question of how it could be. It is essentially problematic.

The idea of the self has been dominated in the West by a dualistic either/or metaphysical framework. On the one hand, there are philosophies such as Plato's, which see mind and body as distinct substances. On the other hand, there are positions such as physicalism (which sees mind as body), and idealism (which sees body as mind). But no matter what, we are ensnared by the dualistic framework, since *mind* and *body* are the key categories, and we either embrace both as independent things or deny one and affirm the other as the independent thing. Even relativists, who see the entire issue as arising out of a chance historical happenstance, remain ensnared by dualism insofar as they merely observe the options and choose one of them.

Faced with such an impasse, the best strategy is to see the problem as due to a false start. Instead of seeing human reality

73

in such either/or terms, we need to devise new categories which see human reality in terms of both/and. Yet this seems to be a blatant inconsistency. For *mind*, that which is private and purposive, is radically different from *body*, that which is public and physical. So any both/and view will be inconsistent, will it not?

Not necessarily. For instance, heat and cold are on opposite poles of the spectrum of temperature, yet they are not divided from each other. Rather, just because they are on a continuum, they can and do blend. This suggests, then, that a way to the both/and solution of the "mind-body problem" is to see the self in particular and the primary category of reality in general as a *bounded continuum*. A bounded continuum is a unique interrelationship between two extremes, where the extremes interpenetrate or asymptotically approach each other, and where there is no inclusive or exclusive ordering of the way the extremes interpenetrate. Heat and cold is one such continuum. The real number series between 1 and 2 is another; for they interpenetrate or asymptotically approach each other, can be ordered in an infinite number of different ways, where any ordering of them will always leave out some (indeed an infinite set of) numbers. So to say that the primary category of self is the mind-body continuum is to say (1) that mind and body themselves are not independent substances but are instead poles of the mind-body continuum, (2) that as poles they are defined in terms of, and so are interdependent on, each other, (3) that there is no one or inclusive ordering of mind and body, but rather (4) mind and body merge or come together in an inexhaustible number of interconnections. Hence, the idea of self as a bounded mind-body continuum takes up the traditional dualistic division of mind and body into a more inclusive framework that displays a range of meanings that imperceptibly blend into each other.[1]

To help focus our discussion, take a particularly hard case of action theory, the question of whether we can go *astray* — of whether we can do wrong knowingly and willingly. We all have a fair idea of what it is to do wrong — concretely, to gull, hurt, maim, rape, kill; generally, not to do what is rational-all-things-considered. And we all have fair ideas of what it is to choose — to take, without coercion, one path rather than another; and what it is to know — to grasp clearly and coherently the essentials of something. But can we put these together? Can we, without coercion, clearly and coherently, do less than what is rational-all-things-considered?[2]

There are three traditional replies to this question — in terms of the self as weak, perverse, and evil. What I aim to show is that all three are required to understand going astray. For each account irreducibly illuminates (1) a way we or others appear when we or they do wrong, (2) a key strategy of moral education, and (3) a primary justification of punishment. Moreover, what makes going astray possible is that the self is a mind-body continuum. For each of the three key concepts that going astray is based on — (1) the self (2) knowingly (3) chooses — will turn out to have an unproblematic and a problematic meaning, where both meanings arise from the mind-body continuum.

I. WEAKNESS

One main account we have of going astray speaks of agents as being weak and thus overcome. This particular view of going astray, made much of by Plato, sees the self in conflict with itself, where one part of the self is of reason and the other against reason, and where the self that is of reason is overcome by the self that is not of reason.

Briefly, reason denotes the practical or theoretical position a person would come to in a given situation when moved exclusively by a consistent, coherent, and complete grasp of the essentials of that situation. That is not to deny the import of emotion and feeling; they would be essential, for instance, in any moral or aesthetic situation. Nor is it to affirm but one position as consistent with reason; it is possible for there to be a number of such positions.

To be overcome, moveover, is not necessarily to be either distraught or horrid. While Plato stresses monster passions overwhelming us, it remains the case that one can be overcome calmly and do nothing terrible. As Davidson observes, I can be overcome when I need to sleep more than I need to brush my teeth and yet "my feeling that I ought to brush my teeth is too strong for me (and so) wearily I leave my bed and brush my teeth."[3] The essential point to being overcome is not that one goes berserk but that one part of oneself proves "too strong" for another part, the rational — what is best for oneself, all things considered.

To understand going astray in terms of weakness is to see that we can be surds to ourselves. As weak persons (1) we see clearly what we should do or be, and yet (2) we do otherwise. In such a case we make no sense to ourselves. But to account for this we must speak of ourselves as having been overcome. Only by seeing ourselves as overcome can we explain why we went against our reason — as not doing what we clearly and coherently see as the best for us to do, all-things-considered. It is in such ways that people overcome by alcoholism, stage fright, and (when exhausted) the need to brush before sleeping see themselves. They recognize overall the absurdity of what they are doing and do it nonetheless.

A second reason for understanding going astray in terms of weakness is revealed by the kind of moral education which treats people as if they are in danger of being overcome. We seek to make their rationality stronger than other reasons they have — for example, particular passions, appetites, and desires — which do not represent their rationality. In short, we try to *strengthen* their fully reasoned point of view by such strategies as shunning, systematizing, and self-discovery. *Shunning* asks agents to recognize that they do not have the power to control themselves in certain situations and thus to avoid those situations. So we urge alcoholics to shun alcohol. *Systematizing* urges agents to take the judgment of their overall rational point of view and intertwine it with a host of diverse insights in order to make their judgment follow from a network of ideas rather than stand by itself alone. So we unabashedly ask alcoholics to overdetermine their reasons for not drinking by relating it to a number of ideas — for example, duty, happiness, role models, creativity. Third, *self-discovery* encourages agents to find out why it is that they act as they do. So alcoholics delve into their past to determine how it is that their reason could have become so dominated by drink. Each of these common and uncontroversial ways of responding to those who go astray is predicated on the idea that their overall reason was overcome and thus requires strengthening.

Hence no matter what wrongs the weak may have done, we have a reasonable expectancy of being able to change them for the better, provided we are able to get their attention. Getting their attention of course may be tricky. It may in fact require an attention-grabbing punishment — as we threaten drunk drivers with jail. Consequently, a third reason for understanding going astray in terms of weakness is that it grounds a standard justification of punishment: punishment is justified to the extent that it is needed to goad the weak into strengthening their reason.

In sum, weakness is an account of going astray because it expresses the three key ideas of going astray — (1) the self (2) knowingly (3) chooses. However, while the first two ideas are unproblematic, the last is not. The first is the normal if extraordinarily complex notion of the *causal* human self — the set of passions, feelings, emotions, appetites, capacities, dispositions, and aims that in part constitute a human person at any given time. The essential idea of the causal self is that its makeup, in some sense or senses, is explained causally. For instance, we explain the self's lack of self-knowledge, and subsequent need for self-discovery, as due to many of its feelings and dispositions being formed early in life and never adequately identified. Moreover, the second idea defining the weak self is a standard notion of knowledge, namely, the clear and coherent grasp of what reason requires.[4] This, then, leaves us with the problem of choice, for to be overcome is not to choose but to be overpowered. What one does merely reflects the outcome of a struggle of diverse internal forces. So what could the weak do about it but, with a horrified fascination, witness it?[5] And why then do we hold them responsible?

The weak are responsible because they can do more than passively observe what happens to them. Above all they can choose to *own* what they do. If they are those kinds of persons who can be overcome, then the nature or character to be overcome is theirs. Moreover, while they can not do much at the moment of being overcome to control directly what they do, they still are indirectly in control of, and so are responsible for, their choices. For, as we have seen, they can choose to *strengthen* their reason. They can choose (1) whether to shun situations where they might lose their capacity to choose, (2) whether to systematize their reason, and (3) whether to engage, by themselves or through therapy, in self-discovery. These choices are indirect in that they do not determine the moment of being overcome, but rather determine secondary events that will avoid, or allow them to better deal with, being overcome. However, they are still our choices and through them we remain responsible.

For weakness to be possible, the self must be both physical and mental. On the one hand, a paramount part of any account of weakness must be physical, insofar as any account must include the causal self, part of which is in conflict with and overwhelmed by another part. The dualistic idea of a substantival pure mind could make no sense either of how the self could be relegated to the status of a mere observer of what is happening to it, or of how it could be so ignorant of what underlies what it does — much like a body tossed by waves in a storm. On the other hand, an equally paramount part of any account of weakness must be mental — in order to make clear the possibility of indirect choice and strengthening. First, one can own what one does and who one is only by self-consciously acknowledging that what one did emerged out of who one is. Merely to *say* that one owns what one did and who one is does not suffice. A rote response is of no significance. To own oneself is to identify with one's causal character and what comes out of it. No android can so own itself. While an android could identify and correct one of its faulty circuits, it could not self-consciously acknowledge the circuit as its own. Second, whether to own oneself, and then, whether to strengthen one's own causal self, are direct choices. In making these choices the self is aware of its alternatives — for example, to drink or not to drink. The choice it makes is the self-conscious living through of one of these alternatives rather than another. To speak of choice in physical terms is thus to change the subject. Hence, no android can choose. While an android can be unpredictable, it cannot self-consciously live through one focus of attention rather than another. Finally, the modes of strengthening — shunning, systematizing, and self-discovery — entail a conscious awareness. For example, in self-discovery, to discover the underlying causes of one's behavior *is* self-consciously to live through how they come from one's past and still enter into one's present.

Consequently, because the self can be overcome, and because the self can be unaware of why it does what it does, the concept of weakness entails some physical basis. But equally so, because owning, choosing to own, choosing to strengthen, and strengthening itself, signify irreducibly conscious acts, the concept of weakness entails a mental basis. The way to bring these two bases together is to reject the traditional dualism/physicalism dichotomy. To reject this dichotomy is to reject dualism, which creates a chasm between mind and body; and idealism, which relies on mind alone; and physicalism, which relies on body alone. It is to take the category of the self to be a mind-body bounded continuum, where mind and body are opposing poles of the same reality. On the one hand, to the extent that it is on the physical pole of the continuum, the mind-body bounded continuum can be caused and so find itself overcome by powers which it only partially understands. On the other hand, to the extent that it partially occupies the irreducibly mental pole of the mind-body continuum, it can also become perspicuous to itself and on that basis make self-caused and so responsible choices.

II. PERVERSITY

Another way to understand going astray, one which harks back to Aristotle, is in terms of perversity. Perversity is a distortion of deliberation, one of the primary kinds of human choice.

As Aristotle saw it, to deliberate is to find out or discover what one's nature, "moving principle,"[6] or reason is. Deliberation thus makes good use of the notion of a causal self. To make a choice is to weigh the causal self's aims and desires and such in order to discover which one most reflects who one is. Who one is then defines one's nature and reason. We all do this, from choosing our favorite ice cream to choosing our career path. For instance, when I decided to become a philosopher rather than a physician, I closely observed my interests and abilities and saw that, overall, they went one way rather than another. This way then came to represent part of my nature and reason.

But what if I had instead become a physician — and solely because my parents had wanted me to? And what if I took this to be what I really wanted? — what I chose? Then I would have come to a position that would not be rational, and yet, at the same time, would be regarded by me as rational. At this point I would be perverse.

The perverse cannot be said to be divided in themselves as

the weak are divided. While the weak see reason and fail to follow it, the perverse wrongly take their nature to represent reason and do follow it. The perverse thus find themselves at one with themselves. They are not, like the weak, a house divided. Moreover, the weak at the moment of being overcome are passive. "Something happens" to them. One part of themselves wins out over reason. But the perverse are active. They find out what their specific nature or reason is, and then follow it.

One main argument for understanding going astray in terms of perversity is that it illuminates another fundamental way we appear when we do wrong. When others do wrong they often appear to us as "beyond reason." For their reason is not considered reason, and so, as Aristotle put it, they are "of necessity without regrets, and therefore incurable."[7] Because the perverse see what they do as rational, there is no standard sense of knowledge, no clear and coherent insight, to appeal to in order to change them. To address the weak we can appeal to reason, for the weak see that what they do when they are overcome denies reason. But to address the perverse, we cannot appeal to reason, for their reason is twisted or bent. To appeal to their reason in order to change them would be absurd, for in their "good sense" they are off-kilter right from the start. Hence Aristotle's despair at finding a cure for the perverse person, "for wickedness perverts us and causes us to be deceived about the starting points of action."[8]

Two other reasons for understanding going astray in terms of perversity are that it provides further strategies of moral education and additional justifications of punishment. In spite of the apparent incurability of the perverse, we do not give up on them. Indeed, many of our most creative strategies in moral education are directed to the perverse. While we cannot strengthen their insight, as we do with the weak, we seek to *reorient* it, and at least in three ways — by retraining, raising, and redirecting.

First, we seek to *retrain* wrongdoers by insisting that their level of behavior meet a minimal level of civilized living. The idea behind this is that how we act in part determines how we reason. Hence, unless people maintain a minimal level of behavior, they have no chance of recognizing what is rational. Thus, we do not take these levels to be arguable points. While we give reasons, the fact that these reasons are not acknowledged or even understood does not prevent us from demanding that these levels of behavior be maintained.

Second, we attempt to *raise* the level of reasoning in wrong-doers by heightening their awareness of how they feel when others do to them what they do to others. So we ask, "What if everybody did that?" and "What if that were done to you?" It is also in terms of addressing the perverse that we uncover further justifications of punishment. Punishment is justified to the extent that it reorients the perverse, first, by retraining them and second, by raising their insight. Finally we work to *redirect* the insight of the perverse by pointing out to them how their bad habits and reasons go against reason.

Of these three ways to address the perverse, redirection is the most problematic. Aristotle, as we have seen, spoke of the perverse as incurable because they cannot be argued with, in the sense of being shown by a demonstration to be in the wrong. Yet, paradoxically, he still argued with them and tried to redirect them. And he was not inconsistent in doing so, for he believed it possible to redirect the insight of the perverse to reason, by showing how their reasoning was skewed.

In order to see how we might redirect the perverse, let us again recall that perversity, as a mode of going astray, is defined by the three key ideas of self, choice, and knowledge. As was the case with weakness, two of the concepts are used in an unproblematic sense. As was the case with weakness, the concept of self is the unproblematic causal self, the self of disposition and aims. As was *not* the case with weakness, the concept of choice is also unproblematic. While the weak do not directly choose to act as they do, insofar as they are mere observers of warring events occurring within themselves, the perverse do directly choose to act as they do, insofar as they find out what their reasons are and act according to them. What is problematic about perversity is its concept of knowledge. For how can the perverse be said to know what they are doing when they fail to see clearly and coherently that what they are doing is not in line with what is rational?

The answer of course is that they cannot. The perverse can no more be said without qualification to know what is rational than the weak can be said without qualification to choose what is not rational. But in a qualified sense they can still be said to know, just as in a qualified sense the weak can be said to choose. For the perverse are ensnared by self-deceit. There is some sense in which they know that what they believe is false. They both believe and do not believe what they are deceived about. It is only in this way that the perverse have a chance of being morally educated for the better.

But how can this be?[9] How is it possible for the self, the very same self, both to believe and not to believe what it is deceived about? An answer requires three steps.

The first is a definition of self-deceit. One is self-deceived if and only if (1) one's own clearly and coherently apprehended rationality conflicts with what is actually rational; and (2) that which is actually rational regularly is present to one's own consciousness. Hence, when one is self-deceived, one directly believes one's own limited rationality, but, because what is actually rational regularly intrudes on one's own consciousness, one believes in an extended sense in what is actually rational.

The second step is to illustrate how considered rationality can regularly intrude on one's own consciousness.

Aristotle argues that we are all at the mercy of ill fortune and cannot reasonably hope to escape it. However, "the man who is truly good and wise, we think, bears all the chances of life becomingly and always makes the best of circumstances," come what may.[10] What allows the "truly good and wise" to bear so well the misfortunes of life is that they have a consolation that the perverse lack. Despite their ill fortune, the good can take solace in their goodness, their rationality, and thereby realize that they participate in a reality that is eternal, godlike. Consequently, the perverse are regularly reminded of the rational. Life is hard. We will of necessity be brought down, by unavoidable misfortune and death. What allows us to endure this well, without the self-destruction of bitterness and fear, is an identification with the good, the rational, which for Aristotle is of cosmic significance. Moreover, while only the good and the rational have this possibility, the perverse need this solace to live well and are repeatedly reminded of this in their everyday life. Hence, the perverse, willy nilly, find the means to avoid self-destruction regularly intruding on their consciousness and yet do not take it. They only "half-believe" it.

Second, Aristotle never accepted ignorance of moral principles as an excuse for going astray. As he remarks concerning "ignorance of the universal" or of the general principles of morality, "for *that* (people) are to be *blamed*."[11] We can be excused for not knowing the particulars of a case. We excuse Oedipus, for example, for being ignorant of who his parents were. But we cannot be excused for being ignorant of general moral principles, for these principles define the common domain of human life and so regularly intrude on our consciousness. Hence they cannot fully escape our awareness. Thus, the perverse in some sense do know them. They "know" them at least indirectly, in an extended sense, as they continually come up against them, whether or not they acknowledge them or make them their own.

Still, none of this explains how self-deceit is possible. For it relies on the metaphors of what is rational "regularly intruding" on the self, so that the self "half-knows," "half-believes," or is "half-present to," what is rational. For the account to make sense, we must take the third step of the argument and unpack these metaphors.

Moreover, by the traditional Western either/or framework, self-deceit cannot make sense. On the one hand, by dualism's count, awareness is of necessity unequivocally present to the self, can in no way hide from itself, and so cannot be self-deceived. If the dualistic self goes wrong, it is either ignorant of its wrongdoing or clearly knows it is wrong. There is no possibility of a middle ground, of a half-awareness. On the other hand, by physicalism's count, self-deceit is equally impossible. For self-deceit entails an irreducible awareness of what we directly know and also of what we indirectly know. While an android could have circuitry that leads it to self-destructive acts, and even a way of repairing its circuitry, and even additional circuitry preventing it from repairing itself, and so on, it would not be self-deceived. To be self-deceived it would have to have an awareness and consequent belief about what it took to be rational, where this awareness and belief were wrong, and where what is rational regularly intruded on its awareness. And these awarenesses and half-awarenesses are just what androids lack.

So the question remains: How is self-deceit possible? What can "half-awarenesses" and the "regular intrusion" of the rational on one's conscious self mean? Since the question appears to be unanswerable because of a dilemma which itself reflects the traditional mental-physical framework, the only way out is to reject the standard either/or of mind and body and adopt a blend of the two—just what the self as mind-body continuum does. The self can half-believe and half-know just because consciousness is not always perspicuous and present to itself. And consciousness need not always be perspicuous and present to itself just because the self is a mind-body continuum which thus entails the possibility of awareness being "in between" the perspicuousness of mind and the torpor of body.

One model that might aid us here is that of quantum mechanics, which holds that there is no answer to the question asking for the precise location and velocity of a micro-particle. Rather, the two are somewhat indeterminate, where the more determinate one is, the less determinate the other is. Likewise, the self as mind-body continuum can be indeterminate. Just as the electron can be in no specific physical position, so the self-deceived self can be in no specific epistemic position. Rather, it can be in between knowing and not knowing.

But how can this be? For if the self knows, then it perspicuously knows—even if it knows itself to be in a haze. Once again, though, such a reply betrays our entrapment in the Great Either/Or—either absolutely perspicuous or absolutely dark. To help us here, consider The Big Beastie Argument.

1. Gonzo, a 600 pound gorilla, is a big beast.
2. To subtract a pound from Gonzo still results in a big beast.
3. What follows, by a series of one pound subtractions from Gonzo, is that Greg the gerbil is a big beast.

This is absurd. Yet which premise do we deny? Surely not the first! But according to standard logic, to deny the second we need a counterinstance. We need to come up with a weight that is heavy and yet which is such that to subtract a pound from it results in a weight that is light. And there is of course no such weight.

The way out of the Big Beastie Argument is to recognize that it employs a vague concept—that of bigness—and that vague concepts have their own kind of logic. In particular, they are not sharp. They speak of a reality that is at times essentially indeterminate and hence do not submit to the clear counterinstances of standard logic.[12]

Further, and of crucial significance, we must learn to work with vague concepts. For vague concepts are most of the time the way matters stand. Most of our important concepts, like that of the self and knowledge, are vague concepts, and it is our task to understand their logic.

Recall, for instance, how we are drowsy. We are neither awake nor asleep but in a daze. And we hazily, dazily, allow ourselves to be so. Or recall how we fall asleep. Just try to go to sleep alertly. It can't be done. Yet I, the self, do go to sleep. And I am responsible for going to sleep. But the "I" here cannot be the I of the fully perspicuous self. For this is not the self that drops off. Nor is it simply the physical self that does this. For choices are being made—even in going to sleep. How impatient we are with ourselves, how we hold ourselves responsible, when we are about to fall asleep and then "choose" to think of something demanding. We don't choose to do this in any direct way. What we do is out of a daze. But we do it and are responsible for it. Or recall how it is that we make some decisions, like getting out of bed in the morning. Sometimes it is the result of a deliberation: "It is now time to rise and shine," we grimly say; and sometimes we simply find ourselves getting up. In the same way we can be in a daze, drift off to sleep, allow ourselves to think of what is demanding, and find ourselves getting up, we also can be unaware in the direct sense, and yet aware in an indirect sense, of what we are doing.

This half-knowledge is neither a capacity nor a potential. We have the capacity to know what our name is, even if we are not thinking of our name; and we have the potential to know what another's name is, even if we never ask or are told. Half-knowing is an active exercise of knowing made possible because *knowing* can be inherently indeterminate just because the self, that is, the knower, is a mind-body continuum.

In conclusion, we have only a weakly justified presumption that we can change a perverse person for the better. While we can appeal to the weak in terms of their clear and coherent insight of rationality, and thus have a reasonable expectancy for their improvement, we can appeal to the perverse only in terms of their having an implicit yet inescapable sense that who they take themselves to be, and what they take themselves to want, runs counter

to rationality. That is, we hope that we may be clever and wise
enough to reorient the perverse to find their way back to the most
justified path, by making clear how this path regularly intrudes
on their consciousness.

The reply is that *freedom* is also a vague term, that at times
it denotes our trying to stay awake. Just as our freedom at times
amounts to choosing not to put ourselves in situations where we
will be weak and overcome, so our freedom is at times found in
the fight to remain alert to the full implications of what we are
doing. Such a struggle is inherently a matter of awareness, as we
seek to stay aware of what we are doing. But it is also inherently
physical, as we are immersed by the torpor of our body. In this
struggle with self-deceit, mind and body interpenetrate. For this
to be possible neither mind nor body can be an independent thing.
Nor can mind or body alone be the primary metaphysical category. Rather mind and body must be opposite poles of the same
continuum. It is because of this that the self is to be understood
as a vague concept, denoting a being that can be drowsy as well
as awake and asleep, that, paradoxically, can non-alertly yet freely
struggle for alertness and freedom.

III. EVIL

The third main account of going astray is the appeal to evil.
The *evil* self purely and simply is that which, without coercion,
and with a clear and coherent apprehension, chooses evil. Here
the self is not mired in conflict, where it is too weak to reject some
lesser but overpowering reason. Nor is the self perverse, not fully
aware of reason. Rather the evil self clear-mindedly apprehends
reason and, without coercion, rejects it. Contrary to the choices
of a good self, it chooses to be characterized by a "reason" that
is anti-reason. Thus, at this level of radical choice, the self is not
moved by any given notion of rationality, whether objective or
merely personal. Rather, the self chooses the reasons on which it
will then act. Indeed, at the level of radical choice, even what constitutes the self's interests hinges on its choices. For considerations
of self-interest presuppose that there is a *chosen* self or nature to
be advanced. Further, one can knowingly choose to go against

one's self-interest as it would be determined by standard criteria. As Milton's Satan puts it:

> Consult how we may henceforth most offend
> Our enemy. . .
> What reinforcement we may regain from hope,
> If not what resolution from despair.[13]

It does not ultimately matter to Satan whether evil succeeds. Only Satan's "will," the brute choice to reject God, counts.

One major reason for understanding going astray in terms of evil is that it illuminates another fundamental way we or others appear when we or they do wrong. At times we refuse to address those who have gone astray as either weak or perverse. Rather, we insist that those who strayed were not only in control of themselves, so there is no need to strengthen their awareness as to what is at stake, but also clearly and coherently grasped what they did, so we have no reason to attempt to reorient their insight in order to align it with what is rational. In other words we see ourselves in situations of radical choice (1) where we are not surds to ourselves, overcome in our weakness; (2) where we are also fully clear about what we are doing, not entrapped by some form of self-deceit; and yet (3) where we nonetheless go against rationality. Such choices are usually portrayed as inherently moral or spiritual, requiring that the self choose between good and evil. But that is not necessary. They can also be prudential. For when I choose, say, whether to exercise, I know that I don't like to exercise, that I am not coerced to exercise, and that it is prudentially best for me to exercise. And yet sometimes I knowingly and without being coerced choose not to exercise — choose not to do what is best, all things considered. At such times we can speak of the self, not as morally or spiritually evil, but, in an extended sense of the term, as prudentially evil. The point is that the self, good or evil, is at times in the strictest sense responsible for its character.

Two other reasons for understanding going astray in terms of evil are found in certain strategies of moral education and justifications of punishment. First, we often appeal to the *power* people have to choose between what is rational and what is not. We appeal to their *radical choice:* we insist that they are responsible for their character. We say that at times one has to choose who one is. We do not allow them to appeal to their nature as an excuse, as if their nature were final, but rather stress that they can choose what their nature will be. This kind of response is particularly applicable to those who claim to be weak, for example, alcoholics, when they are choosing whether to shun alcohol. Then they are not at the mercy of their disease. While their character has been sculpted by genetics, family, and culture, it is not granite hard, and they are not bereft of chisels and hammers of their own.

Moreover, we also use *prophetic passion:* we appeal to their possible goodness and rationality, as we extol the ideal of reason which they could choose. Here we are not appealing to the agent's insight into who he or she is, for we cannot rely on the agent's character being moral or rational. Rather, prophetically, we implore the agent to freely endorse an ideal possibility in human life. We rely on the objective lure of the values themselves.

Finally, we stress that when the evil freely reject moral reality, they must not escape unscathed. Not to punish them is to overlook either that what they did is wrong or that they freely did it. Hence, not to punish them is to tolerate the intolerable, evil and choosers of evil. While punishment of the weak and the perverse is inherently tied to moral education — in the one case getting their attention so that they will strengthen their reason, and in the other reforming their behavior to redirect their reason — punishment of the evil stands as a judgment that evil freely chosen requires retribution. Thus the first two notions of punishment require leniency and compassion in the service of justice and moral education; but the last notion requires a rigid justice alone.

The notion of evil, consequently, has a standard sense of knowledge and it also has a standard sense of free choice. What the notion of evil has difficulty with is its understanding of the self. How are we to understand that which chooses? How can we make sense of that which has no character except the "character" of choosing character?

What comes to mind is the traditional ethereal dualistic entity, a "metaphysical floater" or "soul," that, as Davidson says, performs "mysterious acts."[14] But images are not ideas. How can a nonphysical being do anything? Nor can physicalism help. For physicalism, choice must be understood solely in terms of unpredictability. But unpredictability no more entails freedom of choice than freedom of choice entails unpredictability. An android can be determined by some chance mechanism, some complex algorithm, and so be unpredictable, but that does not mean that the android has free choice. And those with free choice can quite predictably choose the good and right again and again. Rather, freedom is a self-conscious, uncoerced, and knowing living through of one, rather than another, awareness of focus or attention, where this living through of one focus of attention rather than another *is* one's choice. Such choices are no more to be confused with desires than imagination is to be reduced to memory. For a desire is a given: I want to exercise. But a radical choice is a question: What will I do? A desire is part of the causal character; a radical choice is a determination of the causal character.

Thus, in radical choice we transcend our causal self. Dualism has taken this to mean that we must be transcendent beings. Since we do so choose, we must be "souls." Physicalism has agreed with dualism that radical choice entails that there be souls. And then it has concluded that since there cannot be souls, radical choice must be illusory.

Mind-body continuism agrees and disagrees with both. It agrees with dualism, and disagrees with physicalism, in claiming that we do make transcendent choices. It sides with physicalism, and parts with dualism, in holding that there are no transcendent beings. Rather, the self, as a mind-body continuum, is able to transcend its causal character by being present in its mental pole. The person as mind-body continuum finds oneself in this pole when one surveys one's causal self and its alternative causal lines, which make clear what one can do and be. Consequently, not every act or choice is an act of will. Most aren't. The will, or radical choice, plays a role only when we address the normal course of events. It represents a lived abstraction in our lives, as we draw away from the normal causal chain. Moreover, how the self as mind-body continuum places itself in this level of radical choice is itself a long story. We are certainly not, as Sartre claimed, condemned to be free. Most of the time we are not so but are quite content to be in our causal self. Placing oneself in radical choice, like deliberation, must be taught, improves with practice, and is not always appropriate. But in all it has a metaphysical basis, in that it represents an extreme of the self that is the mind-body continuum.

IV. THE ESSENTIAL PARADOX OF GOING ASTRAY

In conclusion, no matter how it is understood, there is a paradox to the question, Can the self freely do wrong? If the same question is posed with each term defined in its standard unproblematic sense, then it reads: Can the self as causal character and as rational, without coercion, and with clear and coherent insight, do wrong? And to this the answer is, No. But this is paradoxical in rejecting what we all know — that we can freely do wrong. Hence, and paradoxically, the question in its unparadoxical sense must be restated to avoid the falsehood that the self cannot freely do wrong. And then we end up with the threefold conclusion that the self can freely do wrong — by being either weak, perverse, or evil. And each of these turns out to be paradoxical. (1) When weak, the self's rationality was overcome. And so, being overcome, it cannot be held directly responsible for what it did. But as a mind-body continuum the self can be held to be indirectly and so paradoxically responsible. (2) When perverse, the self willingly does wrong, but knowingly and only in an extended and so paradoxical sense. As a mind-body continuum it knew what it did, but not clearly and coherently. It knew it only, as it were, in a daze or a haze — through a glass darkly. (3) When evil, it is not the self as causal character that freely goes astray. Rather it is the more paradoxical self as a self-aware choice on the mind-body continuum, which elects to live one option — what is less than rational — rather than another. In all there is much to amaze and astonish.[15]

NOTES

1. For another discussion of this, see Edward W. James, "Mind-Body Continuism: Dualities Without Dualism," *Journal of Speculative Philosophy* 5, no. 4 (1991): 233–55.

2. The terms *rational* and *reason* will be used from now on to mean *rational-all-things-considered* and *reason-all-things-considered*.

Going astray is not the only way the self goes wrong. The self can go wrong *ignorantly*, as Oedipus mistakenly throttled his father and bedded his mother — although it also could be that one's ignorance is due to one's faulty way of collecting and sorting information. The self can go wrong *stupidly*, as, like an oaf, it lacks the intelligence to find out what it should do — although it can also be that its stupidity is a sham, an excuse. The self can go wrong, as Aristotle noted, *precipitously*, without thinking, as a basketball player may throw the ball to the wrong player. Events may happen too fast to allow one to make the right decisions — although it also could be that one has failed to develop the proper steadiness of character and concentration to meet adequately such events. The self can go wrong *accidentally*, as one may quite innocently stumble by a slip of the tongue or a slip of the feet — although, again, it could be that one's accident is the result of the less innocent faults of character like haste or, if we believe Freud, even some neurosis. The self can go wrong *berserkly*, as a deranged person, one physically and neurologically damaged, may run amuck, or less dramatically, may slobber and salivate. In all, then, we have other ways to go wrong. But these cases, clearly, are not the primary ways we go wrong — and even with the first four, as noted in the qualifications, we may be hiding a fault behind an excuse.

3. Donald Davidson, "How Is Weakness of the Will Possible?" in *Essays on Actions and Events* (Oxford: Clarendon Press, 1980), p. 29.

Davidson asks, "Does it never happen that I have an unclouded, unwavering judgment that my action is not for the best, all things considered, and yet where the action I do perform has no hint of compulsion or of the compulsive?"

4. This understanding of knowledge may be seen as having two cases — strong and weak. In the strong case, we see clearly then and there that what we do is against reason — as, for instance, we may find ourselves frozen from fear, or brushing rather than sleeping, but seeing clearly how absurd our (non)action is. In the weak case, we may not see clearly then and there that what we do is wrong, insofar as our passions cloud our judgment; but we still grant and see clearly in general, both before and after the fact, that what is done in these cases is wrong — for example, when we are overcome by a lust or desire.

5. As Davidson remarks, "It is not clear how we can ever blame the agent for what he [or she] does: his [or her] action merely reflects the outcome of a struggle within him [or her]. What could he [or she] do about it?" (Davidson, "How Is Weakness of the Will Possible?" p. 35). How, then, can we speak of the self as choosing when the self is overcome?

6. Aristotle *Nicomachean Ethics* 1110a.

7. Ibid., 1150a.

8. Ibid., 1144a.

9. One way to make sense of this is to divide the self into self-contained compartments, where one compartment knows one thing and another knows its opposite. This would reduce perversity to a kind of

weakness, where one part of the self dominates another. The central problem with understanding perversity as weakness is that it divides the self into a number of selves, each with its own awarenesses and aims. Still, this raises the image of a number of little guys bullying the Big Guy. But what of these little guys? Do they too have self-contained compartments — littler guys in the little guys? If they do, what results is an infinite regress.

10. Aristotle *Nicomachean Ethics* 1100b–1101a.

11. Ibid., 1110b34.

12. See Max Black, "Reasoning with Loose Concepts," in *Margins of Precision* (Ithaca, N.Y.: Cornell University Press, 1970), pp. 1–13.

13. John Milton, *Paradise Lost and Other Poems*, ed. M. Kelley (Roslyn, N.Y.: Walter J. Black, 1943), pt. 1, p. 95.

14. Donald Davidson, "Intending," in *Essays on Actions and Events*, p. 87, n. 2.

15. I wish to thank specifically some of my colleagues and friends for their encouragement and helpful comments on this essay: Barbara Darling-Smith, who was the designated commentator; as well as Charlene Entwistle, Caren Plank, Bill McWeeny, Steven Sanders, David Cheney, and Fran Quaglio.

PART II

Selfhood
in
Various Cultures

The Comparative Study of the Self

ELIOT DEUTSCH

ONE OF THE MOST DIFFICULT tasks in comparative philosophy is to determine whether or not, just because certain similar-sounding terminology is being employed, the same philosophical problem is in fact being addressed in different cultural traditions. This task is particularly evident with problems of the self. The question, of course, is already present in the differing traditions of Western thought. For example, if the Greek *psyche* does not mean the same thing as the English *mind*, the German *geist*, and so on, then in what sense is there a common problem about the self? These traditions, however, do all have their grounding in several common presuppositions and attitudes. Foremost among these Western assumptions is the belief that a person has a special place in nature by virtue of his or her having a mind. From at least Genesis — and then Descartes — we accord ourselves a unique place in the scheme of things, and, despite what many see as the implications of biological evolutionary theory, we continue in philosophy, for the most part, to frame problems of personal identity, the existence of other minds, the relationships of mind and body, and the like, on this assumption of human uniqueness. Sydney Shoemaker has allowed that "it is obvious enough that the existence of a special problem about the nature of persons, and the nature of personal identity, is somehow connected with the fact that persons have minds."[1]

But the problems of the self as formulated in Western philosophy do not often arise in mainline Indian (Brahmanic and Buddhist) thought. The self-consciousness of uniqueness, in the first place, presupposed as we have seen in the formulation of these problems, is missing in favor of an awareness of the continuity of the empirical self and the natural world and the affirmation of the possibility of a radical transcendence of the empirical self. The major problems of the self in Indian philosophy have to do with what is the nature of the empirical or phenomenal self and its relation to other and higher states of consciousness. For Indian Vedantic philosophy, generally, the self or person, in his or her depth, is not identified with the mind — which is usually taken as itself material in nature, the *manas* as another sense organ — but with unlimited spiritual being. The self is identified with Reality itself — however the latter may be understood within its different "schools."

And with Chinese philosophical traditions we are apt to find a still different set of concerns and presuppositions. Problems of the self, for the most part, are governed by ethical considerations. Questions about humankind's "original nature" are indeed asked, but not in search of metaphysical understanding for its own sake, as much as for determining the quality of one's moral consciousness. In the mainline Confucian tradition, for example, the self is taken to be thoroughly social in nature. It is not so much that an otherwise autonomous self enters into relations with others as that she or he is constituted organically by those relations. And hence, for the Chinese, the problem of determining the quality of our inherent dispositions and of allowing for the freedom to realize proper self-cultivation.

We are then compelled to recognize that there are cultural-philosophic presuppositions that largely influence the formulation of specific philosophic problems of the self. These problems, in their specificity, are not universal. I am not aware of any discussions in Chinese philosophy that are quite similar to the "other minds" problem as formulated in Anglo-American empiricist-based thought. I am not familiar with any discussions in Western philosophy, with the possible exception of some materials to be found in the mystical traditions (which most philosophers do not accept as philosophy anyway), which deal extensively with the type of metaphysical questions concerning the status of the individual self (*jiva*) which frequently appear in traditional Indian thought. And so on. Universality is not found at this level of philosophic concern.

Another interesting question arises: Do we have the same philosophical problem in two or more traditions when what counts as a solution to the problem may differ radically? This difficulty is brought out most clearly in the well known Humean/Buddhist parallels. What would count as a satisfying resolution of the problem of the unity of the self for Hume would not satisfy Buddhists. Hume's problem is resolved by his being able, in the face of his denial of necessary connections in experience and his affirmation that experience consists of "distinct existences," to identify that factor which could account for the unity. The Buddha's initial analysis of the self into its constituent elements is similar to Hume. But Buddhism looks for what we might call a "saving answer." Human beings are afflicted with a suffering largely of their own making. This suffering is assuaged by a right view of the self and of other things and a corresponding mental-moral discipline. In Buddhism there is an urgency about the inquiry into the self, and any answer must be therapeutic. Do we, then, have the same philosophical problem?

The answer, I think, is both yes and no — the two being applicable at two different levels of analysis and experience. There must surely be a sense in which differences in presuppositions and differences in criteria of intelligibility and the rest make for a real difference in the very philosophical problems being addressed. Put simply, East Asians, South Asians, Westerners frequently are talking about different things in their various treatments of problems regarding the self. And yet, at a deeper level, we do find that there is a common core of human experience, a range of possibilities that cuts across differences in cultures and indeed differences (gender, class, education, etc.) between individuals in the same culture, a range which gets articulated in diverse ways but which nevertheless serves as a kind of "deep grammar" of experience.

As human beings we share a number of important mental and physical factors which, as brought into patterns of relationship with our world, our environment, disclose similarities as well as differences and enable us to communicate effectively with one another. We oftentimes think we communicate when in fact we do not, but at the same time we could not even come to have that same awareness if we always failed to communicate. And the fact that we do sometimes communicate effectively across cultures in our respective philosophical understandings and analyses of the self suggests strongly that we do share certain basic and central things in common. In any event, this is part and parcel of our philosophical faith. Whereas some anthropologists are pleased at every turn to deny the possibility of universality, most philosophers would find that denial to signal a kind of philosophical death-wish.

Philosophical problems about the self do not lend themselves very easily to isolation from one another and from all the major issues in the philosophy of mind, ontology, epistemology, ethics, and social-political philosophy. If we ask "Who am I?" we realize quickly enough that we are persons who are at once mental and physical, living in complex relationships with our environment and with each other. We are destined, it seems, to perish — and yet while still living we strive to achieve something meaningful for ourselves and contributory to others. We are, in short, knowing, feeling beings who are socially informed, alone and yet always together, quite capable of inflicting great pain upon each other and quite capable as well of acting with extraordinary dignity and grace. This, and so much more, is what it means to be human.

And so where does this leave us philosophically? It seems to me that any adequate theory of the self must strive to be comprehensive and also aware of its own limitations. It must address a multitude of issues concerning the nature of personal identity, the role of the somatic as well as the psychic, the meaning of freedom, and so on — and it should, I think, strive to address these issues in the light of the full richness of human experience, which means, then, cross-culturally. Comparative philosophy, to my mind, is simply philosophy which works in a global context — and this is what, I think, all philosophy should be.

Comparative philosophy has a dual role. We need first of all to *understand*, as best we can, the basic presuppositions, styles of argument, and the rest that are associated with other cultures. This understanding seeks to locate what is truly distinctive in those traditions and to identify what can be contributory to enriched and enhanced philosophical possibilities. This leads quite naturally to the second role, which is the *creative* one of appropriating, in an unself-conscious way, those distinctive contributing elements so as to make them an inseparable part of one's own ground of thought and being. The second task, in short, is simply that of being better philosophers in the light of the understanding of other cultures. For example, one of the most interesting treatments of the self and its identity in Western thought is to be found in John Locke's *Essay Concerning Human Understanding*. His definition of a person at once embodies much of prior rationalistic thought and has been of considerable influence in both later philosophical empiricist thinking and in popular expression. His making of moral responsibility a central part of his treatment of personal identity has also been of considerable importance in Western thought and can be contrasted nicely with the way in which this is accomplished in both classical Chinese Confucian thinking and with mainline Hindu and Buddhist forms of analysis. The contributions of Asian traditions here will, I think, be evident and will be suggestive of new possibilities in dealing with this extraordinarily difficult issue.

After distinguishing between different kinds of identity for different kinds of things — for example, material substances, vegetables, animals — Locke preferred initially a biological criterion of the class-differentiated 'man'. "The identity of the same man," he stated, "consists in a participation of the same continued life, by constantly fleeting particles of matter, in succession vitally united to the same organized body." He then distinguished between the identity of the substance 'man' and the identity of a person, defining the latter in essentially mentalistic terms. A person, Locke says, is

> a thinking intelligent being, that has reason and reflection, and can consider itself as itself, the same thinking thing in different times and places; which it does only by that consciousness which is inseparable from thinking, and as it seems to me essential to it: it being impossible for any one to perceive, without perceiving that he perceives.[2]

Locke goes on to say that

> since consciousness always accompanies thinking, and it is that which makes everyone to be what he calls self, and thereby distinguishes himself from all other thinking things; in this alone consists personal identity, i.e., the sameness of a rational being.[3]

So consciousness, which embodies the crucial power of memory, is the criterion for personal identity. As it has been pointed out, however, "the fact that the same *man* is before us does not mean that the same *person* is."[4] One's actions are one's own only insofar as they are appropriated in memory. This leads to the curious conclusion that, in Locke's terminology, "if a man is not conscious of having performed a certain action then the person did not in fact do it and cannot be held responsible for it."[5] Locke thus "thought it obvious that what makes people accountable for their actions is their ability to recognize them as their own. This seems to mean two things: first, an awareness of what one is doing when one is doing it and, second, an ability to remember having done it."[6]

Let us look at these ideas from the standpoint of some selected dimensions of Asian thought and then see where this might take us toward a richer treatment of the nature of the self and its identity.

It has often been pointed out that Locke's problem of personal identity has been raised in a dualistic context. Most Asian thinking, however, does not work in that context. It rather presupposes some kind or other of mind-body unification. What, then, would the problem of personal identity look like if due attention were given to the somatic as well as the psychic? Considerable attention has been given in recent times to the body, especially by phenomenology, yet I think it is in traditional Indian thought that we get the clearest understanding of the role of the body in personal identity.

According to traditional Indian thought, an individual is very much a result of what he or she does, and what is done more often than not involves the physical as well as the mental. Karl Potter has pointed out that the meaning of *karman* in Indian thought has primarily to do with "making" and not with "acting" as such, as we have come to employ that concept in contemporary action-theory.[7] And in the last analysis it has to do with self-making. Who I am is how I make myself and my world; it is the manner in which, by virtue of accumulated experience, I am predisposed to continue the patterns and structures of that experience into the future. Individuals are habituated beings and thus become bound up with their own doings and makings.

An individual's identity, then, is assured across time, for every individual has a unique psychophysical history of his or her own making. What a person is qua individual is very much a part of what she or he karmically performs. Actions are always one's own, with respect to what is done and how they are done. *Karman*, in short, constitutes the core of individuality.

And how surprising it is to sometimes discover that the body seems to have its own repertoire of actions, its own remembered behavior. Who has not done something — such as ride a bicycle — which one hasn't done for many years, only to find, after a very short time, that one "remembers" how to perform the particular action? The body, too, has its *samskaras*.

The more central contribution, however, that this whole thinking about personal identity and *karman* makes philosophically, is in understanding how persons get constituted physically through what I would call an *appropriation* of their physical conditions of their being. This idea of appropriation will in turn contribute significantly to the idea — developed in its own way in traditional Chinese thought and missing conspicuously in Lockean accounts of the self — that a person is an achievement and not a mere given of nature.

To "appropriate the physical" means that one has fully acknowledged the given physical conditions of one's being, and that one has selected from among them those that are educated for specific forms of disciplined action. Appropriation means bringing the physical, as well as the mental, into the full fabric of one's sense of self. Gabriel Marcel said that the body can never be exterior to our central reality of ourselves. A person does not simply say that "I am my body" nor does he or she say "I am not my body"— for the body as appropriated becomes one of the very conditions of self-identification.

Locke, and others after him, entertained the idea that personal identity could be sustained entirely in mental terms; in other words, that one could maintain an identical *I* in different bodies. But if we are at all correct in our understanding of body appropriation, then it is simply not the case that a person is contingently related to his or her body. The person is the psycho-physical being that has been shaped by experience and cannot be as such except in those terms.

This does not mean, however, that a person is fixed for all time. Quite the contrary, it suggests that a person is only achieved as an ongoing phenomenon. Locke would have us believe that a person just is insofar as a bare memory of past experience obtains. But it seems to me that we persist as persons to the degree to which we are what we ought to be within the conditions of our given individuality. I will not go into the "ought" here, but only indicate what bearing this has on moral responsibility.

In his rather bizarre extension of Locke's thinking on per-

sonal identity, Derek Parfit had argued that a person is responsible for her actions only to the degree to which she has retained
causally strong links and continuities with her past selves.[8] According to Parfit, we are persons only by degrees — not qualitative in
achievement terms but quantitative in terms of memories and other
retentions. One is simply not responsible, he argues, for deeds carried out a long time ago, for one is simply not the same person
who carried out those deeds and who is now embarked on other
adventures.

Alasdair MacIntyre, on the contrary, has argued — and I think
rightly so — that

> I am forever what I have been at any time for others — and
> I may at any time be called upon to answer for it — no matter
> how changed I may be now. There is no way of *founding* my
> identity — or lack of it — on the psychological continuity or
> discontinuity of the self. The self inhabits a character whose
> unity is given as the unity of a character.[9]

We are then, thoroughly responsible for what we do and have done,
for we are our makings and can never be dissociated from them.

This leads us to a further consideration regarding the self and
its identity — and one that is also rather conspicuously absent in
much empiricist-based Western thinking, namely, the self as *social*. MacIntyre went on to say that

> the story of my life is always embedded in the story of those
> communities from which I derive my identity. . . . The posses-
> sion of an historical identity and the possession of a social
> identity coincide.[10]

In Chinese philosophy we cannot even conceive of an individual or person as being apart from others, for the whole range
of relationships between an individual and his or her world is socially mediated. The language that one has learned from others
within a culture enters into the very fabric of one's perceptual experience. The manner in which one does what one does is throughout informed by societal conventions and expectations. A person,
quite clearly, is a bearer of a culture as well as a creative participant in it.

This leads us to the related problem of autonomy and freedom. A great deal has been said in Western thought about autonomy, with the differing views each representing different conceptions about the self. We may, in a very sketchy way, sum this up with reference to several dominant ways of thinking. First is the general Greek understanding of the autonomous person as self-governing through the exercise of reason, which exercise enables him to control the passions, harmonize otherwise conflicting dimensions of his nature, and, especially for Aristotle, realize himself socially as a participant in the *polis*. The autonomous (*autonomos* ["self-law"]) person is thus one who achieves the fulfillment of humankind's proper end — that of virtue thoroughly informed by reason.

With the development of seventeenth- and eighteenth-century liberal-democratic thinking, we see a shift toward a more atomistic, individualistic view of the person. Human beings are bearers of "rights" in relation to the state, so that the *autonomous* meant primarily the independent and, as far as possible, the self-sufficient. The autonomous person was one who, employing intelligent judgement, was free to pursue his or her own happiness without unnecessary interference from other persons or the collective society.

Romanticism, on the other hand, with its emphasis on neither reason nor reasonableness, but on the will, spontaneity, and imagination, saw the genius of the paradigm of autonomy. It was the creative artist who was the genuine law-giver to himself. Not everyone was, could be, or (for Nietzsche) should be autonomous. Whereas for the Greeks everyone (that is, male citizens) was in principle capable of being rational; and for liberal thinkers everyone was equally endowed with certain unalienable rights; for the romantic only a privileged few could enjoy anything approaching the power of genuine self-governing and expression.

There are, of course, other important views about the self and autonomy, principally in our time those informed by Marxist thought and psychoanalytic theory, but the general sense of autonomy as independence, whether universal or particular, seems to persist.

But Asian thought often gives a very different picture. For example, in classical Confucianism the *chun-tzu*, translated by David L. Hall and Roger T. Ames as the "authoritative person," is precisely one who is thoroughly grounded in the social and yet realizes true humanity (*jen*) through the achievement of a certain style of acting and being. The autonomous person, if the expression were allowed, would be the self-disciplined, social person who was able spontaneously to know what was the right thing to do in any particular situation. Being properly attuned, as it were, and in openness to others, the authoritative person is what he or she is by virtue of competency. To act autonomously means, then, to act with skill, in harmony with self and others.

In this, and in related Indian views, there is little concern with notions of independence. Rather there is the deep recognition of the many ways in which human beings are interdependent and interconnected. To acquire the skills necessary for self-realization one obviously needs to be educated by others; and psychologically as well one needs others to acquire a sense of one's own worth and dignity.

This suggests further that an adequate conception of autonomy involves the understanding that when one is autonomous one does perform actions in a certain way; namely, one performs actions freely.

It is characteristic of much Western thinking about freedom, especially since the rise of modern science, to locate freedom in the will and then see this freedom in the context of a causally determined world of natural events and happenings. Uniformity of causality rather than its universality is stressed, except among those who would deny freedom altogether in favor of a strong determinism running through all events, natural and human. What is characteristic, on the other hand, of much Asian, especially Indian, thought is the locating of freedom not in the will but in consciousness, with a corresponding emphasis upon the universality of causality rather than upon its nomic uniformity. Freedom thus becomes a rare achievement, for it calls for the realization of a qualitatively different mode of consciousness, one that is transcendent to that ordinary sense-mental consciousness which is thoroughly bound up with habits and self-makings (*karman*).

One thing which is suggested by this view, and which may help us to resolve many of the apparently insuperable problems associated with the freewill/determinism controversy, is that freedom can be seen as an inherent quality of a person and his or her action and not just as a possible condition for a certain kind of morally responsible act. To act freely means to act spontaneously in such a way that the act exhibits a certain rightness relative to the kind of act it is and the special conditions of the individual actor. I am free when and insofar as I am able to attend to reality, to listen to its vital rhythm, and to embody that attentiveness, that listening within the concrete forms of disciplined action. Actions are free when they attain a quality or style of grace which expresses one's own true being. Freedom itself can then be understood as that which, when achieved, is simply native to a person and his or her acts.

Problems of the self are among the most intractable in philosophy and we can be quite certain that no one thinker, school of thought, or tradition will provide answers that are definitive and enduring. Experience changes; new ways of conceiving ourselves appear; and indeed different ways of understanding our relation to others, to the world, to spiritual being will always be brought forth. And that is the glorious task of philosophy.

NOTES

1. Sydney Shoemaker, *Self-Knowledge and Self-Identity* (Ithaca, N.Y.: Cornell University Press, 1963), p. 8.

2. John Locke, *An Essay Concerning Human Understanding* (London: George Routledge & Sons, 1689), p. 246.

3. Ibid., p. 247.

4. Terence Penelhum, "Personal Identity," in *The Encyclopedia of Philosophy*, ed. Paul Edward (New York: Macmillan and the Free Press, 1967), vol. 6, p. 97.

5. Locke, *An Essay*, p. 248.

6. Locke, cited in Penelhum, "Personal Identity."

7. Karl Potter, "Metaphor as Key to Understanding the Thought of Other Speech Communities," in *Interpreting Across Boundaries: New Essays in Comparative Philosophy*, ed. Gerald James Larson and Eliot Deutsch (Princeton: Princeton University Press, 1988), pp. 19–35.

8. See Derek Parfit, *Reasons and Persons* (New York and Oxford: Oxford University Press, 1988).

9. Alasdair MacIntyre, *After Virtue* (Notre Dame, Ind.: University of Notre Dame Press, 1981), p. 202.

10. Ibid.

The Dignity and Indignity of Service: The Role of the Self in Hindu Bhakti

JOHN B. CARMAN

MANY IN THE WEST have thought of India as the home of Eastern wisdom, a wisdom at whose heart is a conception of the self as a single mysterious reality behind all the multiplicity of natural phenomena, a reality that underlies the trillions of souls animating all living beings. Behind all finite selves is the one true Self. Within all the many souls there is the one "Oversoul."

As our acquaintance with Indian thought increases we learn that there have been many diverse conceptions of the self. There is the notion of the invisible but still material soul known as the "subtle body," and there is the belief in the soul as the agent in ritual and moral action. There is the Jain notion of a vast plurality of purely spiritual souls that can with great effort be scrubbed clean of their material bodily connections, and there is the Buddhist denial of the reality of any enduring substantial entity, whether finite or infinite, that matches the common misconception of the soul.

Even within the school of Hindu thought known as the Vedānta, from which two centuries ago Europeans made their generalizations about Indian wisdom, there are some crucial differences. The monistic interpretation of the school of Śankara differs from the interpretations of those who were involved in a series of movements, singing, dancing, and acting out what is called *bhakti*, which means both devotion to God in a personal form and sharing in the life of God with a community of devotees.

The earliest evidence of such Hindu devotion comes from the Tamil-speaking South of India beginning about 400 B.C.E. The particular group with which we are concerned are those who wor-

ship Vishnu as the Supreme Lord, together with his Divine Con-
sort Lakshmi. They concern us both because they continue to use
in their worship hymns composed between around 600 and 800
C.E. by a group of Tamil poet-saints and because they claim to
incorporate the orthodox tradition of Vedic learning, including the
summation in the Vedānta philosophy of the discourses at the end
of the Vedas called the Upanishads. Their most famous teacher,
Rāmānuja, whose traditional dates are 1017 to 1137 C.E., is honored in the community of his followers, largely in South India,
and also respectfully remembered by devotees of Lord Vishnu in
other parts of India. He is known in the history of Indian philosophy for his theistic alternative to Śankara's monistic interpretation of the Vedānta. He was also engaged in other disputes, however. Perhaps the most important of them was his dispute with
conservative Brahmans about the validity of the Bhakti stance
toward the goal of human life and the means to attain it, a dispute that centered on my topic: the dignity—or the indignity—
of service.

I have chosen to focus on Rāmānuja because he is the Bhakti
thinker with whose work I am best acquainted. I started out to
write a dissertation on Rāmānuja's doctrine of divine incarnation.
In the course of that writing and in my subsequent studies I have
become more and more aware of the interconnections between his
philosophical thought and the other dimensions of his religious
heritage. These include temple ritual with its sacred images and
its music, the double heritage of Sanskrit and Tamil scriptures
that his community claims to combine in their "dual Vedānta."
There is also the ongoing problem of realizing the moral ideals
of Bhakti in a community dominated by Brahmin men but also
containing many members of lower castes, including the untouch-
ables who have been the virtual or actual slaves of South Indian
society. The Brahmin scholars transmit a tradition that honors many
non-Brahmin poet-saints and especially remembers among them
an out-caste singer and a woman devotee whom the Lord united
with himself, and the greatest poet, Nammāḻvār, who in many of
his poems took the role of a maiden in love with Lord Vishnu.

After some exploration of many of these contexts of Rāmānuja's thought, I have recently returned to a text that was important in my first study and to which I now turn.

The final section of Rāmānuja's *Vedārthasaṃgraha* starts in the manner of many Indian philosophical works with an objection or contrary opinion that must be refuted in order to reach the final conclusion. In this case, however, the objection cited is not a philosophical one but a quotation from the most prestigious collection of Hindu law, the Laws of Manu. This objection follows an important statement describing devotion (*bhakti*) as a kind of love (*prīti*) and a kind of knowledge (*jñāna*), knowledge which is bliss (*ānanda*) because its object is Ultimate Reality (Brahman), who is absolute and eternal bliss. This statement concludes with the sentence: "All this means that the person who has Brahman as the object of his knowledge becomes happy."[1] Rāmānuja then continues as follows:

> The Supreme Brahman, treasure store of countless superlatively auspicious qualities, is flawless, possesses the infinitely great realm manifesting his glory, and is an ocean of superlatively gracious condescension (*sauśīlya*), beauty (*saundarya*), and motherly love (*vātsalya*), is the master (*śeṣi*), and the self is the servant (*śeṣa*). When the Supreme Brahman is meditated upon in that relationship, and as the object of superlative love (*prīti*), He therefore causes that self to attain Him.[2]

At this point comes an impeccably orthodox objection:

> What you have said would mean that the state of being absolutely in the position of servant (*śeṣa*) is the soul's superlative happiness, but that is a conclusion opposed to the world's experience, for we see that what is desired by all intelligent beings is nothing else than independence or self-dependence (*svātantryam*) and that dependence on someone or something else (*pāratantryam*) is more painful [than independence]. Moreover, Manu states, "All dependence on others (*parāvaśam*) is unhappiness; all self-dependence is happiness," and likewise, "Service is called a dog's life, so abandon it."[3]

It is highly significant that at the end of the only philosophical work in which Rāmānuja was free to arrange the sequence of objections and objectors, he saves to last the task of answering an objection that claims to be both worldly wisdom and an injunction from Scripture: Service is an unpleasant state, so abandon it.

Rāmānuja's reply forms the conclusion of the *Vedārthasaṃ-graha*. The desire for independence comes, he says, not from the soul but from the body; it is a desire to experience a certain kind of bodily pleasure. However, the soul's proper nature, which is consciousness, is distinct from the nature of all kinds of bodies, and it is also the soul's nature to be in the relation of subservience (*śeṣa*) to God. Both of these definitions of the soul or finite self are based on a host of scriptural texts. The alternative ideal of the soul's independence is, Rāmānuja maintains, a misconception of the soul caused by karma; that is, a false identification of the soul with some particular body. The true meaning of the text "All dependence on others is unhappiness," Rāmānuja goes on, is that the self is in this relation of subservience (*śeṣa*) *only* to the Supreme Person; hence service to anything or anyone else than God *is* unhappiness. Likewise, "Service is a dog's life" properly refers only to service to one who is unworthy to be served. Only the Supreme Person is worthy to be served by all who know the true nature of the soul, and that service is described by Scripture as a knowing (*vedana*) of God that has the form of supreme devotion, which is the way to attain God. God must choose to save, and God chooses those who are most beloved (*prīyatama*), in whom superlative love for God has been generated.[4]

I have followed the scholarly tradition of the last hundred years in translating the Sanskrit term *śeṣa* as "servant" and the abstract noun *śeṣatva* (or *śeṣata*) as "subservience." This term and the corresponding word for owner or master (*śeṣin* or *śeṣī*) recur frequently in all Rāmānuja's writings and may well be the most important and distinctive technical terms that Rāmānuja employs. This is especially true in this work, which is Rāmānuja's statement of his theology without the need to fit it into the predetermined sections of a commentary. These terms are among the few that Rāmānuja takes the trouble to define, and they are metaphysically important because they form one-third of Rāmānuja's definition of his most celebrated metaphysical doctrine: that the relation of Ultimate Reality to all finite realities is like that of the finite self or soul to its body. This Ultimate Reality is Brahman, the Supreme Self and Lord (*Īśvara*). The self-body relationship consists of three highly unequal relationships: between the support (*ādhāra*) and what is supported (*adheya*), between the controller (*niyantā*) and what is controlled (*niyāmya*), and between the principal part (*śeṣī*) and the accessory (*śeṣa*), which third relationship can also be expressed as that between the master or owner and the servant or property.

It is this third relationship with which I am chiefly concerned here, and I have to begin with the obvious difficulty of finding the right English term to convey the meaning that Rāmānuja found in *śeṣa* and *śeṣī*. The difficulty is not that we do not know the earlier Sanskrit meanings or even that Rāmānuja does not define the terms, but rather that by the end of Rāmānuja's fairly elaborate discussion of the *multiple* meanings of *śeṣa*, it is clear that the most literal meaning, "remainder," will not do. Yet it is not clear which of the derived meanings is most appropriate. If we vary the English translation according to the context, we lose the importance of *śeṣa* and *śeṣī* as technical terms.

The original meaning survives in the negative form, *aśeṣa*, "without remainder" and hence "entire," but in its use in the *Karma Mīmāṃsa* the term also meant "subordinate part" or "subsidiary" and was used in the sense of "accessory" to characterize any subordinate part of the sacrifice that is instrumental to its principal goal. Thus *śeṣa* is defined in the *Karma Mīmāṃsa Sūtra* as follows: "one constituent is *śeṣa* when it is subservient to another."[5] The *śeṣī* is that which possesses or is characterized by a *śeṣa* and hence is "the principal element to which other elements are *śeṣas*."[6] While Rāmānuja's explicit discussion of *śeṣa* is in the context of debate with the Prābhākara School of Karma Mīmāṃsa, he clearly had in mind a definition in Sanskrit grammar that moves even further away from the original meaning: "*Śeṣa* is an object possessed, whereas the possessor is the *śeṣī*."[7] Thus Rāmānuja's own definition in the *Vedārthasaṃgraha* goes as follows:

> The *śeṣa* is that whose essential nature consists solely in being useful to something else by virtue of its intention to contribute some excellence to this other thing, the *śeṣī*. . . . The essential nature of born slaves (*garbhadāsa*) and other servants is solely that they are beings who have value for their master (*puruṣa*) by virtue of their intention to contribute some particular excellence to him.[8]

In my book *The Theology of Rāmānuja*, I concluded that in this discussion in the *Vedārthasaṃgraha* "God is the owner and master, and all his creatures are in the position of slaves."[9] I went on to note that the similar discussion in the *Śribhāṣya* also recognizes that the *śeṣī* is "not simply the beneficiary of the actions of his servants; he also acts for their benefit."[10] At that point I commented on this two-sided benefit being interpreted as two-sided responsibility in Vedānta Deśika's *Rahasyatrayasāra*: intelligent beings are obligated to serve their master, but it is also the owner's responsibility to protect what belongs to him.

Not until recently did I see any reason to dissent from the scholarly consensus of translating the relation of servant to master as "subservience." Indeed it seemed a happy medium between "servitude," which suggests the indignity of slavery, and "service," which does not necessarily include the drastic subordination of the servant to the master. One advantage of the form *śeṣa* is that it can be used either personally or impersonally to mean "servant," "property," or "instrument." That is indeed important, but I am now convinced that it is still more important that the terms *śeṣa* and *śeṣī* enable Rāmānuja to talk about two apparently opposite sides of a fundamental metaphysical and personal relationship: to talk about both the indignity and dignity of service.

This is a *re-vision*, quite literally. I now think that I *see* something that I failed to see before, something so obvious that it stares me in the face and I wonder why I never noticed it.

Before I let you in on my very modest discovery, let me mention a couple of things I had already noted in comparing Rāmānuja's more strictly philosophical works with his commentary on the Bhagavadgita and with his prayer of surrender or "taking refuge," the *Śaraṇāgatigadya*.

Rāmānuja elaborates his predecessor Yāmuna's theistic interpretation of the Vedānta, the Hindu effort to systematize the teachings of the Upanishads. All of the interpreters recognized the apparent discrepancy or even contradiction between different scriptural statements concerning the unity of the cosmic Brahman and the distinction between Brahman and the cosmos. Whether the major types of later interpretation all go back to the beginning of this school of thought is unclear. In any case Yāmuna and Rāmānuja argue against two alternative positions. One, called "Difference and Non-difference," sees reality as alternating in vast cosmic cycles between a compacting of all reality within Brahman and an emanation of finite reality out of its infinite source. The

other, of which Śankara is the outstanding representative, adopts
a two-level view of reality. The lower level does not seem very different from Rāmānuja's universe presided over by a personal Lord,
but that lower view of the reality of a manifold and variegated
universe distinct from Brahman appears false, once one has awak-
ened to a higher level of consciousness. The finite universe is then
discerned to be like a magician's trick, real only so long as you
remain under the magician's spell, and Brahman is intuited as the
one and only reality, the Self identical with one's own self.

Rāmānuja accepts as axiomatic both a distinction and a connection between the Infinite Self and all finite selves. Finite selves
share in reduced measure the reality and joyous self-consciousness
of the Supreme Self. Thus Rāmānuja can affirm Upanishadic definitions of the self as applying to both the Supreme Self and finite
selves. In addition, however, it is necessary to have a relational
definition that clarifies the radical subordination of the finite to
the infinite. Thus Rāmānuja affirms both the metaphysical basis
of the universe of infinite and finite spirits and the distinction necessary for worship.

There is a story in the traditional biography that suggests that
at one time Rāmānuja remembered only the Vedāntic definition
of the self and forgot this second relational definition of the finite
self as the Lord's servant. It is said that Rāmānuja was dictating
the *Śrībhāṣya* to his disciple Kūraṭṭālvān (Kūreśa), to whom he
had given permission to stop writing if he heard anything with
which he did not agree. When Rāmānuja defined the finite self
(*jīvātmā*) as *jñānaikasvarūpa* (whose essential nature is wholly
consciousness, or that which has cognition alone as its distinguishing attribute),

> Kūreśa ceased writing, for to him such a definition, though
> valid, was as good as no definition, inasmuch as the most es-
> sential characteristic of the soul, namely its *allegiance* or *liege-
> ship* to God, *śeṣatva*, was a serious omission; . . . for no basis
> for true religion was raised by merely apprehending the soul
> as *that which is characterized by consciousness*, unless the
> soul is also the *sole property* or possession of the Universal
> Soul, God. Defining soul as *that which has consciousness
> merely*, without any reference to its being essentially related

to God, as quality is related to things, or as property to a base, or as mode to substance, as light to the sun or scent to the flower, amounted to tacitly ignoring such essential relationship; and that without this relation to God first emphatically asserted and defended, anything said of the soul was ineffective, inasmuch as a soul without God is nonexistent, in the same way as without the sun, light is nonexistent. . . . But Rāmānuja was absorbed in his thoughts; and continued dictating further but Kūreśa had come to a full stop. This incensed Rāmānuja, who cried: —"Sir, if *you* wish to write the commentary on the *Vyāsa-Sūtras (Brahma Sūtras)* you may do so," and kicked him and ceased dictating. . . . Rāmānuja by the time, reflected over the whole position in his retreat; and it flashed on him that his omission to define the soul as *that which is belonging of God* was a grave mistake inasmuch as the essentiality of soul was the very foundation of theology.[11]

For those who know that one Tamil word for servant literally means "foot" and that the poet-saints referred to themselves when singing to the Lord as "I am your foot (*aṭiyen*)," the irony of Rāmānuja's using his feet to kick his faithful and discerning scribe would not have been lost.

At first glance Rāmānuja's comments on the verses of the Gītā seem to push the doctrine of one-sided dependence even further. In that commentary Rāmānuja even makes a distinction between the finite self's relation to its body and the Supreme Self's relation to his cosmic body. Although the soul is superior to the body, there is some mutual dependence, for the soul also depends on the body to accomplish its purpose. God, however, is not similarly dependent on the cosmos or on the souls within the cosmos. Rāmānuja paraphrases Krishna in Gītā 9.4–5:

> My existence (*sthiti*) is not under their control, which means that they are not helping in any way in My existence. . . . I am the supporter of all beings; they are no help at all to me at any time. . . .

Nevertheless, God's love for his finite devotees (the *jñānīs*) is so great and his longing so intense that God declares that he also needs them to sustain his Divine Self (*ātmā*). We see this in Rāmānuja's comment on 8.14 and even more emphatically on 7.18. "I consider that the *jñānīs* are my very self. This means that the support for my existence is under their control." In Gītā 9.29 Rāmānuja goes even further:

> Those who worship me out of intense love because they cannot sustain their souls without worshiping Me exist within My very self provided with every happiness as though their qualities were equal to mine. "I, too, am in them" means: I treat them as if (*iva*) they were my superiors.

That little word *iva* is all that separates Rāmānuja's position from the less qualified language of later Śrivaiṣṇava tradition, which puts the paradox flatly: the Lord is dependent on his dependents. Note that it is some of the apparently monistic verses of the Gītā that Rāmānuja interprets, not as affirming a unity beyond personal distinction but rather as suggesting what other verses have denied, the appearance of mutual dependence between the Infinite Lord and finite beings.

In this respect Rāmānuja's Prayer of Surrender seems less radical and closer to the earlier tradition of devotional hymnody in both the vernacular Tamil and classical Sanskrit, but Rāmānuja draws on an older Sanskrit hymn of the community for a new word for service, *kainkarya*, which is derived from a phrase meaning, "What may I do for you?" Such eager anticipation of the opportunity to serve the Infinite Lord is regarded, not as a means to some goal beyond menial service, but as the goal itself. This desire to serve the beloved Lord appears as the constant refrain in this type of devotion, even more important than confessions of one's weakness and sin, or yearnings for the Lord's sustaining presence, or glimpses of divine bliss.

Now we should go back to the work with which we started and to its very first lines, which are a so-called *mangalaśloka*, an "auspicious verse." Such a verse is intended to express in an elegant poetic form the central teaching of the work to follow. As with most poetry, we need both to *listen to* the *sounds* of the words and to *look at* the *images* suggested by the words. When I first studied this verse more than thirty years ago, I was impressed with Rāmānuja's ingenuity in suggesting so much of the content of his teaching in so few words, but I did not pay enough attention to the poetic form. I did not listen and look. The verse in Sanskrit sounds as follows:

> śeṣa cidacidvastuśeṣine śeṣaśayine
> nirmalānanta kalyāṇanidhaye viṣṇave namaḥ

This may be translated into English as follows:

> Obeisance to Vishnu, who is the treasury of auspicious quali-
> ties, which are infinite and untainted by any impurity, who
> is the Śeṣī of all entities without exception, both spiritual and
> material, and who reclines on the primordial serpent Śeṣa.

Note first that the *sound* śeṣa occurs three times in the first short Sanskrit line. *Aśeṣa* means literally "without remainder" and thus comes to mean "without exception" or "completely." Śeṣī is the mas-ter or owner of the śeṣas. The third śeṣa we have not yet discussed. This is Anantaśeṣa or Ādiśeṣa, the Infinite or Primordial Śeṣa, the cosmic snake on whom Lord Vishnu reclines in the milk ocean. Why is this living couch supporting the Lord called Śeṣa? The lit-eral meaning of "remainder" may be connected with the notion of the great snake as some kind of cosmic emanation or incarna-tion. In any case, for Rāmānuja and his followers this great snake was certainly an exemplary "servant." The pun on the word śeṣa is indeed a pun, but one that is intended to suggest more than just the artistry of the author. Given the importance of the concept of śeṣa in the middle and at the end of the work, we should cer-tainly look carefully at the relation of Lord Vishnu to this special Servant.

Keeping in mind this image of Śeṣa supporting the Lord, think again *visually* about Rāmānuja's definition of the soul-body rela-tionship. In the first part of the relationship the superior reality supports all the inferior reality; the Lord underlies souls as souls underlie their bodies. In the second part of the relationship, the superior reality controls the inferior one, and this is imagined as control from within: the soul *within* the body, the divine "Inner Controller" within the soul. Now look at the third part of the re-lationship; it seems the reverse of the first, for the Śeṣa literally lies beneath and supports the Śeṣī. We might think that this one

"Infinite Śeṣa" is an exception, but listen again to Rāmānuja's general definition of śeṣa:

> The śeṣa is that whose essential nature is just to be useful to something else by intending to contribute some excellence to that other superior reality, the śeṣī.[12]

It is true that the śeṣa is subordinate to the śeṣī, but the śeṣa is not the passive recipient of support. It has something of its own, valuable though finite, to contribute to the superior reality of which it is an instrument or subordinate part. Both the *sub* and the *servient* are accurate in defining the position of the śeṣa, but the present English meaning of *subservient* leaves out what is so evident if we remember the figure whom Rāmānuja names in the first line of his treatise. *Subservient* leaves out the *dignity* of the servant.

During the last several years I have become increasingly interested in the relation of Rāmānuja's prose theology to the poetic sources of his distinctive vision of reality. I had thought that Rāmānuja's metaphysical interpretation of the Vedānta was the part of his thought most governed by the effort at rational consistency, whereas in the sphere of devotional experience Rāmānuja comes much closer to the paradoxes of the tradition before and after him. I now wonder whether such a distinction within his thought is justifiable. Indeed the paradox of the superior sustaining reality accepting the gifts and the assistance of the inferior reality being sustained is very close to the paradox hinted at in Rāmānuja's commentary in the Gītā and boldly affirmed by Rāmānuja's followers: the Lord is dependent on his dependents.

Because the Lord is self-sufficient he does not need his devotees' sacrificial offerings, according to Rāmānuja's interpretation of Krishna's words in the Gītā, yet the Lord does need his favorite devotees, not to add to his external wealth but to sustain his own inner self.

Here in the *Vedārthasaṃgraha*, however, Rāmānuja is not speaking about *exceptional* devotees but about the basic metaphysical constitution of reality that makes possible significant relationships, one dimension of which is service. In the theology of some of Rāmānuja's successors, the Lord's grace is so total and the Lord's ownership so complete that there is no longer the possibility in this earthly life for the devotees to offer anything to the Lord, even their own souls. Rāmānuja, however, believes that the Lord expects the gifts and welcomes the service of finite beings, each with their own distinctive excellence to contribute to the divine nature.

Some Concluding Reflections

My exploration of the meaning of service in Hindu devotion has been deliberately narrowed to one distinctive term in one philosophical treatise. I have briefly noted other terms and other texts of Rāmānuja's, and I have directed attention to a significant image from nonphilosophical literature: the primordial serpent Śeṣa, lying on the milk ocean when the universe is in a state of dissolution, forming a bed for Lord Vishnu to lie on in a state of sleep or yogic trance.

In his recent book on Rāmānuja's thought, Julius Lipner has tried to deal with the problem of whether the soul has moral worth only if it is conceived, not merely as totally dependent on and controlled by God, but also as completely subservient to God. His interpretation of the concept of *śeṣa* itself certainly stresses the *śeṣa's* subservience:

> The born servant, by compliantly accepting his natural serving-function, and by acting accordingly, exalts his master for what he is — the master — by functioning as what he is, the servant. Whether we approve of natural servitude or not, the example brings out what Rāmānuja understood by the principal-accessory relationship: that by duly expressing its nature the accessory glorifies its principal — it throws the spotlight, as it were, on its principal, not on itself.[13]

Lipner goes on to say that "in the realm of value discourse . . . one appreciates the value . . . of the accessory . . . only in terms of the principal."[14] Ultimately, we derive our value and dignity as persons in our capacity as servants, as accessories, of Brahman the supreme Value."[15] Lipner recognizes the problem that Rāmānuja does not seem to be according any value to the soul: "Brahman alone is that end in terms of which all other ends derive their worth. How then can we say that the *jīvātman* is an end-in-itself and that it is an intrinsic value bestower to the world?"[16]

Lipner answers this question by pointing out that "in the principal-accessory relation's finite application, the individual *ātman* [self] is assured that it is an end-in-itself, a value bestower in its own right, through its relationships with its material body."[17] In other words, Lipner emphasizes that souls are finite masters of their own bodies as well as finite servants of their infinite Master. With this I certainly agree, but I now am able to argue that the concept of servanthood (*śeṣatva*) itself contains an affirmation of dignity or value as well as a recognition of subservience.

One meaning of service is glorification, in Rāmānuja's view. This means that the servant adds to the glory of the one served by contributing to its particular value. This can be put in terms of the nonpersonal or physical meaning of *śeṣa*. Rāmānuja assumes that jewels enhance the beauty of the wearer. There is a value in even the tiniest gem, not indeed as an "end-in-itself," but as an appropriate instrument to contribute to the beauty of the necklace and hence to "magnify" the beauty of the person whom the necklace adorns. For Rāmānuja the value of material things is genuine and significant, even if we consider this value "only instrumental." Both this sullied finite universe sustained and controlled by the Lord's free creativity (*līlā*) and the realm of permanent (*nitya*) enjoyment are called *vibhūti*, finite realms of glory adding to the luster of their infinite Owner and Master.

Rāmānuja was a Brahmin man leading a community in which other Brahmin men constituted most of the intellectual and cultic leadership but in which there were many active Brahmin women participants and an undetermined number of lower-caste participants, probably including a number of untouchable devotees. Professor Rāmānujan has pointed out that the stress on the humility of service is characteristic of high-caste male devotees. It is they who stand highest in the Hindu social hierarchy and whose pride most needs to be shattered if they are to serve the Lord. Their attitude is well represented by Rāmānuja's hypothetical objector who quotes from Scripture: "Service is a dog's life, so avoid it."

The close connection in social reality between *servant* and *slave* certainly suggests that the language of service will have a different ring when it is used by a Brahmin than it does when used by an untouchable. A similar problem affects the modern Christian concept of service for those who are in social circumstances

where they or their ancestors have had no choice but to be servants, serfs, or slaves and who have suffered the indignity of such
compulsory servitude.

Hindu devotees of low caste as well as high caste have been
willing and even eager to consider themselves "slaves of God."
Within the Śrīvaiṣṇava community the word *dāsan* (Tamil masculine form of the common Indian term for "servant" or "slave") is
often added to a man's name at his initiation ceremony and used
thereafter on formal occasions. The feminine form of *dāsī*, moreover, suggests the status of the favored devotee Āntāl, who in one
poem imagines herself in an intimate love relation with the Lord.
In a still more famous poem she leads the cowherding women of
Lord Krishna's village of Braj in a ritual act of service to the Lord
whose external form is a prayer and dance for rain but whose hidden meaning, according to the commentator, is union with Krishna.
This is a still more desirable and intimate service that Āntāl may
have uniquely realized during her physical existence but that all
devotees of the Lord may aspire to in the heavenly estate.

Within the community Rāmānuja's followers do consider
themselves servants of one another. One substitute for the first person pronoun *I* literally means "I, who am your servant," and when
Śrīvaiṣṇava men greet one another with *aṭiyen dāsan*, this increases
the rhetoric: "the I who is a servant is your servant." This might
be compared with the Victorian closing of a letter used by British government officials, "I remain, sir, your most obedient and
humble servant." This brings us to some question of comparison
in the modern Indian situation, and perhaps the world situation.
In the secular world where all are supposedly equal, all may serve
and be served without indignity. Even cars are serviced. Christian service, on the other hand, is intended to acknowledge the
indignity and the potential humiliation of serving those beyond
our family and kin group who need our help. The dramatic effect
of the Christian nursing profession in India, most publicly represented by Mother Theresa, is that it confronts what is still considered the indignity of service, not because of a modern secular
affirmation of equality but because it follows a divine example of
both service and humiliation. This Christian ideal of humble service is close enough to the Hindu theology of God's gracious condescension to lead many modern Vaishnavas to follow Gandhi's

program of service to the whole village, including village servants.

Rāmānuja's point in his debate with conservative fellow Brahmins appears to be much more limited. What would be an indignity in relation to other human beings, as Rāmānuja argues in the *Vedārthasaṃgraha*, may well be a dignity if one has the opportunity to serve the Divine Master.

Even so, it is worth noting that Rāmānuja makes much less use of the common term for *servant* (masculine *dāsa* and feminine *dāsī*) than of this obscure term *śeṣa*. Then he supplements *śeṣa* in his liturgical works by the more emphatically positive concept of *kainkarya*, which we might translate as "eager service." Moreover, Rāmānuja is working from a vision of reality in which materiality embodies or even "clothes" or "adorns" spirituality with a great variety of excellent features. The audience he is addressing in his Sanskrit writings is a Brahmin elite, but it is precisely that elite which knows that he speaks on behalf of an intercaste community of fellow servants of God. In any case his message is clearly that his hearers will miss the truth and their own salvation if they regard themselves *only* as conscious beings who enjoy the service of their material bodies. In relation to the Supreme Master *they* are *śeṣas*, subordinate yet able to make their particular contributions to the cosmos that is the body of God. They participate in an ongoing offering of gifts that contribute to the adornment of the Lord. If not in this life, then in the heavenly life to come they can look forward to experiencing fully the dignity of service as they share in the divine presence. In this life such experiences of God's presence are fleeting, but they can take comfort in what they share with all finite beings, even the primordial serpent Śeṣa: the dignity of service.

That original cosmic serpent is incarnated with Vishnu as his brother and boon companion Balarāma. Rāmānuja's followers believe that Rāmānuja himself is also a reincarnation of that original Śeṣa, the exalted yet humble servant of God.

NOTES

1. Rāmānuja *Vedārthasaṃgraha* 242.
2. Ibid., 243.

3. Ibid., 244.

4. Ibid., 250–51.

5. *Karma Mīmāṃsa Sūtra* 3.1.2.

6. Ibid.

7. Rāmānuja *Vedārthasaṃgraha* 121–22.

8. Ibid.

9. John B. Carman, *The Theology of Rāmānuja: An Essay in Interreligious Understanding* (New Haven and London, Conn.: Yale University Press, 1974), p. 149.

10. Ibid.

11. Alkondavilli Govindacharya, *The Life of Rāmānujāchārya* (Madras: S. Murthy, 1906), pp. 135–36; cf. Ramakrishnananda, *Life of Rāmānuja* (Madras: Sri Ramakrishna Math, 1959), pp. 187–88.

12. Rāmānuja *Vedārthasaṃgraha* 121–22.

13. Julius J. Lipner, *The Face of Truth: A Study of Meaning and Metaphysics in the Vedantic Theology of Ramanuja* (Albany: State University of New York Press, 1986), p. 132.

14. Ibid.

15. Ibid., p. 133.

16. Ibid.

17. Ibid., p. 139.

Selfhood and Spontaneity in Ancient Chinese Thought

LIVIA KOHN

THE OBJECT SELF AND THE OBSERVING SELF

THE PSYCHOLOGIST ARTHUR DEIKMAN makes a distinction between what he calls the "object self" and the "observing self." This distinction for him is fundamental for separating ordinary consciousness from the mystical mind.

I will use the same distinction to clarify the understanding of the self in ancient Chinese thought, in the Taoist and Confucian traditions in particular. I shall argue that the distinction between the object self and the observing self applies to the dichotomy between what in classical Chinese is called "selfhood" and "spontaneity."

The Taoist tradition expresses the dichotomy in a distinction between human beings and the Tao, between ego-centered mind and pure spirit, between the personal body and the cosmic body. Ancient Confucianism, on the other hand, makes a distinction between the ego-centered self and the fulfillment of socially determined roles, the mind that is concerned only with individual desires, and the selfless realization of one's function in the world.

What, then, is the object self? How does it differ from the observing self? And where are we as individual selves placed in this scheme?

The object self, according to Deikman's theory, is first of all part of the natural evolution of human consciousness. At birth, the human world is nothing but a blur of confusing sensual impressions of varying kind and intensity. In the first phases of life, people use their bodies as templates to understand the world. Their

123

primary experience is based on the senses and expressed in physical needs or desires. The first rudiments of a self develop between these two. An object perceived with the help of the senses is understood in its own nature through the body. A first abstract, yet humanly fundamental, concept emerges: object = body = self.[1] One's very own body, the agent that processes the sense data and translates them into needs and desires, is seen as an object in itself.

Consciousness of the object self can be divided according to three distinct functions: thinking, feeling, and acting. The thinking self contains one's conception of who and what one is. It is a "me" defined by society and culture; it includes all the characteristics one attributes to oneself: tall, ugly, strong, shy, and so on. Thinking is bound by relativity and the dependence of opposites. It is based on measurements and comparisons, on the establishment of categories and classifications.

The feeling self contains the emotions: anger, fear, worry, sadness, joy, and so on. All these are reactions of feeling toward a given object or objective. They are intimately linked with desire. I am joyful because something I have desired has actually happened; I am anxious lest something I desire now will not develop; and I am sad or angry because some object of my desire has passed away. The feeling self is the self of desire; it classifies the world according to whether it is desirable or undesirable at any given moment and reacts with feelings and emotions accordingly.

The acting or functional self contains all that we do. It is an awareness of oneself as an acting individual. I know that I do; I realize the capacity I have to act in the world. I feel my body as an instrument of outer activity; I direct my feet and hands, my facial muscles, as well as my vocal cords, in a particular direction, producing a particular effect. The acting self manipulates the world around it. It pulls objects and objectives toward it or pushes them away.[2]

These three taken together constitute the object self. What thinking, feeling, and acting have in common is their conceptual basis in the world and the self as objects to be evaluated, classified, and manipulated in certain ways. They constitute the hard core of the ego in the center of a person, a core that is the measure of all things, yet always remains an object itself.

There is, to begin with, nothing wrong with developing a healthy sense of self-preservation and conceiving of the world and oneself as objects. In fact, it is a necessary stage of human development, an evolutionary phase that is essential for survival of both individual and culture. On the other hand, as children develop, so evolution proceeds further. The vision of the world and oneself as objects eventually becomes only one of several possible modes of self-conception. Robert Kegan distinguishes six such modes, of which only the first three are object-centered. From them, the individual develops to a greater acceptance of and respect for other human beings, to stages of mutuality, harmony, and a fruitful interindividual vision of life and the world.[3]

Arthur Deikman acknowledges the same development when he speaks of another mode of consciousness that people learn to develop over time. This he calls the "receptive mode," a way of perception which diminishes the boundaries between self and world and gives people a sense of merging with the environment.[4] An example of this would be the appreciation of a piece of music or a work of art. Looking upon anything artistic as a mere object one is bound to be bored by it, left cold and untouched. In order to appreciate art, people must open themselves to it and merge with it, to a certain degree. The same holds true for more intense relationships among people. No true understanding can take place if individuals keep themselves shut into a world of mere objects.

The observing self, then, is the fulfillment of the receptive mode. Originally at the center of one's being, this self is the deep inner root of one's existence, an ultimate and transcendent sense of being alive within. It is there, yet cannot be consciously known, felt, or manipulated: it cannot be objectified in any way. Rather than thinking, feeling, and doing things actively and with regard to an object, the observing self allows things to happen spontaneously. People then see themselves and the world as flowing streams of energy, intensely alive and perfectly individual, yet ultimately interconnected in a cosmic whole. The observing self has no limits; it is transcendent and yet most deeply immanent in all.

The observing self as Deikman describes it is in many ways similar to Abraham Maslow's concept of Being-cognition. Being-cognition is the opposite of Deficiency-cognition. Where the latter is constantly aware of something missing, something needed, the former is content and calm — receptive, as it were — and merely observing.[5] Being-cognition allows a wholeness of perception that is in itself enriching. Maslow claims that the more someone learns to perceive and act without deficiency-determined purposes and remains free from value judgments, the more beautiful, meaningful, and good the world becomes to this person.

Although perception in the receptive mode of consciousness is unifying and free from classification, thinking still takes place; but, instead of clear-cut value judgments and the evaluation of things as objects, there is now a sense of fluidity of values, an openness to other points of view.

Similarly, there is still feeling, but there are no emotions that are intrinsically related to the desires of the ego. In a state of Being-cognition, Maslow says, "the only possible emotions would be pity, charity, kindliness, and perhaps sadness or Being-amusement with the shortcomings of the world."[6]

Also, people in this state still can and do act in the world. But their actions are not based on single-minded categorizations nor on ego-centered emotions. They act for the good of others, they do a job well for its own sake, and in general they give others' needs precedence over their own wishes.[7] As Deikman emphasizes,

> There is no solution to the problem of meaning except to transcend the motivations of the object self. The path to that transcendence is service — real service, which means serving the task and, ultimately, serving what mystics call the Truth.[8]

Both Arthur Deikman and Abraham Maslow agree that, although naturally inherent and spontaneously available to human beings, the receptive mode of consciousness has to be learned. It develops only through actively overcoming the values and reaction patterns of the object self. Part of a person's inner being, the observing self or Being-cognition are yet not gained without an effort. The object self, the sense of Deficiency, is a necessary and inevitable stage in the development of an individual human being. It has to be passed through and controlled if true receptivity is to be found.

SELFHOOD AND SPONTANEITY

In ancient Chinese philosophy, both the Taoist and the Confucian understanding of the self bear out the fundamental distinction Deikman and Maslow make between the two fundamental modes of perception. Most basically, it is expressed in the different words used for "self." In modern as well as classical Chinese, "self" is *ziji*, a term that consists of two characters. These two characters, although frequently used interchangeably and both indicating "self," connote the two different visions of the self: a vision of an organized and object-oriented selfhood (*ji*) versus one of a self-contained and receptive, if only gradually realized, spontaneity (*zi*).

Both words for "self" are radicals in the Chinese writing system, which means they are basically meaningful parts of the Chinese language. *Ji* ("selfhood") is written 己; its more ancient form is 己. The graph originally represents "the warp and weft of a loom" and shows "two threads running transversely and another running lengthwise."[9] From its very beginning, *ji* therefore shows an organized structure, something one can see on the outside, something that can be made and controlled.

Beyond its meaning of "selfhood," the character is used already in oracle bone inscriptions as the sixth of the ten earthly stems, a group of ten characters which were used to indicate the names of the ten-day week in the Shang dynasty. As sixth stem, *ji* is associated with the center of things and later with the cosmic phase Earth. It is the organized, structured center of the world; it is what one thinks of as self.

Grammatically *ji* is used primarily in the object position. One can "right one's selfhood";[10] one can "conduct oneself";[11] one can compare others to one's self;[12] one can search for humanity or virtue within it.[13] *Ji* as the self is therefore an object among other objects; it represents an organized person among other people. In this latter aspect, the word often is contrasted with *ren* 人 (literally, "people") but often merely indicates others. "I shall not let the fact afflict me that others (*ren*) do not know me (*ji*)," Confucius says repeatedly.[14] And he formulates the Golden Rule using the same contrast: "Do not do unto others (*ren*) what you would not wish done to yourself (*ji*)."[15]

In the same vein, *ji* is often explained through and used similarly to *shen*, 身 "the personal body." This word, whose pictogram shows a human figure with a protruding belly, like *ji* occurs as a pronoun indicating oneself as opposed to others.[16] Also like *ji*, the personal body is a constructed and organized object, something that develops and grows, not something one is equipped with spontaneously.

Very clearly Taoist texts contrast the personal body (*shen*) with the more spontaneous and less psychologically determined physical body (*xing* 形). Where the physical body refers to the basic physical endowment of a human being, to the "shape" or "form" one's body has in this world, the personal body includes the psychological identification of oneself with one's body. The physical body is a basically cosmic entity: it represents heaven, earth, the four seasons, and the five phases in miniature. The personal body, on the other hand, is a human construction: it consists of all the likes and dislikes, passions and desires, needs and emotions that an individual ego develops toward the objects of the world. In this sense, the term *personal body* connotes the object-oriented, organized self, otherwise expressed by the word *ji*.[17]

Both Taoist and Confucian thinkers assert that this humanly made and object-dependent selfhood has to be adjusted, subdued, cultivated, or destroyed altogether. "To subdue the self (*keji*) and recover proper ritual constitutes humaneness," Confucius says, and he continues: "If a person can, even for one day, subdue his self and recover proper ritual, all under heaven will recover humaneness through him."[18] Similarly the "Great Learning," a chapter of the *Book of Rites* and one of the famous "Four Books" of neo-Confucianism, sees the key to human development in cultivating the personal body (*xiushen*) 修身.

> In the old days those who wished to make bright virtue radiate throughout the world would begin by putting their states in good order. To put their states in good order they would first harmonize their families. To harmonize their families, they would first cultivate their personal bodies. To cultivate their personal bodies, they would first make their minds sincere.[19]

The *Daode jing*, first and foremost among the texts of philosophical Taoism, is somewhat more radical. It finds the personal body an outright affliction to life and a major obstacle to one's attainment of the Tao.

The reason why I have great afflictions
Is that I have a personal body.
If I had no personal body,
What afflictions would I have?[20]

That the personal body here indicates the object-oriented self-hood and not the physical body is made very clear in a later interpretation:

"Not having a body" does not refer to not having this particular physical form. It rather means that the bodily structure is unified with the Great Tao, that one is never influenced by glorious positions and does not seek after speedy advancement. It is to be placid and without desires.[21]

In the same vein, the *Daode jing* insists that a true sage should always disregard oneself and put oneself in the background,[22] that one should withdraw oneself as soon as one's work is done.[23] More strongly than this, the *Zhuangzi* even pleads for the complete dissolution of all selfhood: "The perfect man has no self!" as the text states emphatically.[24]

What is left when the organized self is dissolved or fully cultivated is the other type of self, the *zi*. This term indicates an individual's spontaneous inner being, the qualities one is endowed with by nature. Like the physical body, the spontaneous self is cosmic. It is the way one is spontaneously, the natural so-being of oneself, the way nature or heaven has made people before they develop ego-consciousness and desires for objects.

The graph for *zi* 自 goes back to the pictogram 𦣹, which shows a human nose.[25] The nose is the most protruding part of the face and as such is a person's central characteristic. Still today, people in East Asia point to their noses when they want to indicate themselves. And yet the nose, however much it represents oneself, cannot be seen or known. One can only guess at the shape of one's own nose with the help of a mirror. It is something one is equipped with by nature, something one feels and uses, but cannot shape or control. The nose, as the center of oneself, is part of one's basic makeup; it points back at one's natural so-being, at the spontaneity of one's existence.

Grammatically *zi* is used exclusively in the reflexive position, that is, before the verb. It never occurs in the object position.[26] Whatever one does, if done by the *zi*, is done of itself and by the self as a spontaneous, independent organism, not by an organized object-centered self. In this sense, the *zi* can give rise to an inner feeling of shame;[27] it can have a spontaneous inclination toward good or bad fortune;[28] it can develop spontaneous knowledge[29] or attain true spontaneity within.[30]

The word *zi* in its reference to spontaneous so-being is most clearly present in the compound *ziran* 自然, literally "self-so," but commonly translated as "nature" or indeed "spontaneity." As such, the expression *ziran* is sometimes also used to refer to the spontaneous part of the self. In Confucian texts the term denotes the given nature of the individual, that within a person which is not artificially constructed or controlled.[31] In Taoist documents, on the other hand, *ziran* is immediately linked to the Tao, to its independence and the absence of all relationships. "Heaven patterns itself on the Tao, and the Tao patterns itself on the self-so," says the *Daode jing*.[32]

Beyond that, the term indicates the spontaneous activity of all creatures, a way of being themselves that brings them most closely to the Tao. The true person in the *Zhuangzi*, free from evaluations and personal feelings, "just lets things be the way they are (*ziran*) and does not try to help life along."[33] By remaining in nonaction and free from thinking, feeling, and acting, everything will move along spontaneously.[34] There will be nothing that is not done.[35]

The dichotomy between an organized, conscious, and object-oriented selfhood that has to be suppressed or cultivated, and the true spontaneity of nature within, pervades the understanding of the self in the ancient Confucian and Taoist traditions. In both cases, the spontaneous so-being of nature within a given human being functions like the observing self or like Being-cognition. Originally present in the depth of the human psyche, it yet cannot be known, felt, or manipulated as an object. Overlaid increasingly by a mode of consciousness that centers on outer objects and expresses itself in egoistic desires, the spontaneity of nature is hidden under an organized selfhood, a personal body that is dependent on outside stimulation and comparison for its very existence.

Only through hard work and prolonged efforts at cultivating and subduing object-oriented selfhood can the spontaneity of nature be attained. There is no avoiding this task. The organized self-hood or personal body is a necessary and inevitable stage of human development that everyone has to go through. In fact, were it not for the existence of the ego-centered self, neither Confucianism nor Taoism would have anything to teach to the world. Both philosophies instruct their followers to find the "True Way"— true humaneness for the Confucians, oneness with the Tao for the Taoists. Both emphasize the difficulty of the undertaking and the obstacles to be overcome. Spontaneity, although part of inherent human nature, is not easy to realize. It is the endpoint of long and arduous training.

This training, then, in accordance with the different Confucian and Taoist visions of the ideal human state, proceeds differently and leads to different results. As I have described variously, Taoists strive for a harmony with nature, a going-along with all-that-is, an inner resting in nonaction, a mystical union with the Tao.[36] Confucians, on the other hand, aim for a smooth and harmonious society, a selfless fulfillment of social roles, a spontaneity within the framework of cosmically sanctioned hierarchies and social structures. In the latter case, the dichotomy between selfhood and spontaneity is sublimated into the opposition between individual desires and social harmony.

INDIVIDUALITY AND SOCIAL ROLES

The teaching of Confucianism has dominated much of Chinese society for nearly twenty-five hundred years. It is not surprising, therefore, that the Confucian effort to develop and perfect people's social awareness, and to control their personal desires, has been recognized as one of the major characteristics of traditional Chinese culture. Numerous studies have accordingly drawn attention to the fact that there is no true problem of the individual self in ancient China. Questions like "Who am I?", "What am I?", or "Why am I?" are not asked. As Wolfgang Kubin points out, there is no sense of critical self-reflection, nor is there the true tragedy of an individual faced by an irresolvable dilemma.[37] For Rolf Trauzettel there is even no *I* as "self-identical substance," no self as a "fundamentally singular and independent entity."[38]

Wolfgang Bauer's studies of Chinese autobiography document the point. Although an ancient and varied genre, Chinese autobiography does not encourage critical self-questioning or self-analysis. The earliest autobiographies merely consisted of short summaries of a person's life. They were extremely schematic and made much use of comparison with traditional models. The individual emerges only as the conglomerate of different standardized patterns. Later, in the Song dynasty, a more complex and much longer kind of autobiography developed in the form of chronological self-descriptions. Still, the predominant mode was a stereotypical description of the person, emphasizing his or her relation to classical models, not individual idiosyncrasies. Critical evaluations and questioning searches of the self do not appear before the contact with Western culture.[39]

Another example of the same tendency toward stereotype and the predominance of established models is the literary self. Chinese literature does not dwell on quests for self-knowledge, on extended self-pity or self-mortification. Rather than facing severe moral choices, the protagonist of traditional Chinese fiction, as Joseph Lau has shown, only has to follow the lessons of the ancients. His or her given social situation always provides the only possible way of action.[40] A hero who — in ignorance of the fact — was raised by the man responsible for exterminating his entire family has no qualms whatsoever in killing his benefactor when he learns the truth. His social position as a member of his original family precedes his gratitude to his adoptive father. A self-questioning does not take place; the social role determines his behavior and, one presumes and hopes, his feelings.

At the same time, characters who show some critical or assertive individuality tend to be villains and outsiders. They are shown to be self-obsessed, causing their own destruction by pursuing their egocentric desires.[41] Positive heroes, on the other hand, practice self-denial for the sake of a larger good, be it the Tao, the world, society, or just the fulfillment of duty.[42]

The same rejection of independence and the individual in favor of community and social coherence is also found in traditional Chinese law, as it developed in the Confucian state. As Rolf

Trauzettel documents, the law was entirely aimed at restoring social harmony after a breach; therefore it only determined punishment in regard to the severity of the disruption and disregarded whether the deed was done with or without harmful intention on the side of the perpetrator. The individual did not count — only his or her impact on the whole of society.

The same attitude is also evident in the high emphasis placed on confession in criminal proceedings. Wrung, if necessary, from the accused by force and torture, the confession was the essential testimony that a breach in social harmony had occurred and, at the same time, the first step in healing that breach. Its importance lay not in proving the guilt or innocence of anyone involved in a crime, but in the need to heal the network of social harmony.[43]

The high regard for social harmony is the concrete expression of the particular Confucian training and indoctrination that aimed primarily at the dissolution of the ego-centered self in favor of an understanding of oneself as a social figure, a servant to society and the world, a part of a larger whole. Confucius himself has described his efforts as a continuous process of lifelong learning,[44] and his followers have never tired of pursuing, in W. Theodore de Bary's words, "a self-realization in which man fulfills all that is distinctly human while participating in the creative work of heaven and earth."[45]

Thus, as Tu Wei-ming has shown, adulthood in Confucianism means an unceasing progression of "becoming human." In the end, after seventy years of effort, one can finally "follow one's heart's desire without transgressing the boundaries of right."[46] To be fully human in this context means to have internalized the rites and rules of society to such a degree that one goes along with them spontaneously. The organized ego that had to learn, the self that related to society as an object among other objects, is dissolved. Society, the cosmic order, and the individual self are integrated into one great harmony. The "joy of a childlike heart," as Mencius describes it,[47] the simplicity of spontaneity, is found in the complete integration of self and society, in the harmonization of what one is and what one ought to be. The aim of Confucian cultivation is thus "to quiet down or curb selfish desires, while directing active emotions toward unselfish ends."[48] Thus social and universal harmony is realized.

This harmony ultimately means a loss of the individual selfhood in favor of a larger unity; it means giving up personal
thoughts, feelings, and actions. The individual is gradually freed
from the object relationship to self and world; desires are dissolved;
emotions are lessened; the will of the ego is loosened. Where there
was an ego-centered, selfhood-oriented will before, now all willing is based on something higher and larger. As Herbert Fingarette
describes the phenomenon,

> While the will that I direct toward the Way is personal re-
> garding its initial locus of energy, and control over the arousal,
> intensity, direction, and persistence, when it comes to the
> *ground* on which I choose and justify the direction for my
> will, and on which I elect to maintain that will vigorously
> and wholeheartedly, that ground is in no way one that has
> reference to me personally.[49]

The very same concept, somewhat more cosmologically oriented,
is also voiced in the commentary to the *Zhuangzi* by Guo Xiang
of the third century. He says,

> This life of mine, I did not bring it forth. Thus all that occurs
> throughout my life of perhaps a hundred years, all my sit-
> ting, getting up, walking, and staying, all my movements, all
> my quiet, all hurrying and resting of mine — even all the feel-
> ings, characteristics, knowledge, and abilities I have — all that
> I have and all that I don't have, all that I actively do and
> all that happens to me: it is never me, but principle only.[50]

The vocabulary changes. Where the Confucians emphasize
the importance of the rites and social harmony, the Taoists stress
principle and the Tao. Still, the structure remains the same. Self-
realization in ancient China meant the dissolution of the ji and
the development of the zi, the giving up of selfhood in favor of
spontaneity, the end of the object self and development of the observing self.

The Confucian tradition is highly concerned with society and
social integration; thus its criticism and disregard of individual
selfhood seem stifling to us and a form of bondage. The Taoist tradition strives for the immediate link of humanity and the cosmos;
it encourages the dissolution of the self for the Tao and the spon-

taneity of nonaction. Thus its rejection of ego-centered selfhood seems mystical to us and a form of liberation. Nevertheless, both are part of the same overall tradition; both deny the limited ego of the object self and favor the wider openness of the observing self. They both strive for cultivating and subduing selfhood in favor of spontaneity.

NOTES

1. Arthur J. Deikman, *The Observing Self: Mysticism and Psychotherapy* (Boston: Beacon Press, 1982), p. 68.

2. Ibid., pp. 92–94.

3. See Robert Kegan, *The Evolving Self: Problem and Process in Human Development* (Cambridge, Mass.: Harvard University Press, 1982).

4. Deikman, *The Observing Self*, p. 71.

5. Abraham H. Maslow, *Toward a Psychology of Being* (New York: Van Nostrand Reinhold, 1964), p. 83.

6. Ibid., p. 82.

7. Deikman, *The Observing Self*, p. 112.

8. Ibid., pp. 114–15.

9. Edoardo Fazzioli, *Chinese Calligraphy: From Pictogram to Ideogram: The History of 214 Essential Chinese/Japanese Characters* (New York: Abbeville Press, 1986), p. 34. See also Leon Wieger, *Chinese Characters* (New York: Dover Publications, 1965 [originally published in 1915]), p. 217.

10. *Mencius* 2a.7. For a translation of the Mencius, see James Legge, *The Four Books: Confucian Analects, The Great Learning, The Doctrine of the Mean, The Works of Mencius* (Taipei: Chengwen, 1971 [originally published in 1892]).

11. *Analects* 5.15 and 13.20. For a translation of the *Analects*, see Legge, *The Four Books;* Arthur Waley, *The Analects of Confucius* (New York: Vintage Books, 1938).

12. *Analects* 1.8. The notion of a significant other is central to the Confucian understanding of the self. All individual identity is found primarily in relation to others, especially one's parents and immediate social superiors. See Tu Wei-ming, "Selfhood and Otherness in Confucian Thought," in *Culture and Self: Asian and Western Perspectives*, ed. Anthony J. Marsella, George DeVos, and Francis L.K. Hsu (New York and London: Tavistock Publications, 1985), pp. 131–51.

13. For a detailed grammatical description of *ji*, see W. A. C. H. Dobson, *A Dictionary of the Chinese Particles* (Toronto: University of Toronto Press, 1974), pp. 414–15. A discussion of *ji* in the *Analects* is found in Herbert Fingarette, "The Problem of the Self in the *Analects*,"*Philosophy East and West* 29, no. 2 (1979): 131.

14. *Analects* 1.16, 4.14, 14.3, 15.18.

15. *Analects* 12.2.

16. Dobson, *A Dictionary of Chinese Particles*, pp. 599–600.

17. For a study of the body in Taoism, see Livia Kohn, "Taoist Visions of the Body," *Journal of Chinese Philosophy* 18 (1991).

18. *Analects* 12.1.

19. For a translation of the "Great Learning," see Legge, *The Four Books*, as well as Wing-tsit Chan, *A Source Book in Chinese Philosophy* (Princeton: Princeton University Press, 1964). For a discussion of self-cultivation in Confucianism, see Donald J. Munro, *The Concept of Man in Early China* (Stanford: Stanford University Press, 1969), pp. 91–96.

20. *Daode jing*, chap. 13. For a translation of the *Daode jing*, see Chan, *A Sourcebook in Chinese Philosophy*, pp. 137–76.

21. "Inscription on Sitting in Oblivion." See Livia Kohn, *Seven Steps to the Tao: Sima Chengzhen's Zuowanglun* (St. Augustin/Nettetal: Monumenta Serica Monograph 20, 1987), p. 114.

22. *Daode jing*, chap. 7.

23. *Daode jing*, chap. 9.

24. *Zhuangzi* 2.1.22, following the concordance edition, *Zhuangzi yinde* (Taipei: Hongdao wenhua, 1971). For a translation of the *Zhuangzi*, see Burton Watson, *The Complete Works of Chuang-tzu* (New York: Columbia University Press, 1968) as well as A. C. Graham, *Chuang-tzu: The Seven Inner Chapters and Others Writings from the Book of Chuang-tzu* (London: Allan & Unwin, 1981). A discussion of the self in the *Zhuangzi* is found in Judith Berling, "Self and Whole in Chuang Tzu," in *Individualism and Holism: Studies in Confucian and Taoist Values*, ed. Donald J. Munro (Ann Arbor: University of Michigan, Center for Chinese Studies, 1985), 101–20.

25. Fazzioli, *Chinese Calligraphy*, p. 29; Wieger, *Chinese Characters*, p. 325.

26. See Dobson, *A Dictionary of Chinese Particles*, p. 751.

27. *Analects* 12.23.

28. *Mencius* 2A.4.

29. *Zhuangzi* 4.2.27.

30. *Zhuangzi* 15.6.5.

31. See Richard van Houten, "Nature and *tzu-jan* in Early Chinese Philosophical Literature," *Journal of Chinese Philosophy* 15 (1988): 35–49.

32. *Daode jing,* chap. 25.

33. *Zhuangzi* 15.5.58. *Nature* or *spontaneity* is generally a central term in the *Zhuangzi.* See A. C. Graham, *Disputers of the Tao: Philosophical Argument in Ancient China* (La Salle, Ill.: Open Court Publishing Co., 1989), pp. 186–92.

34. *Zhuangzi* 56.21.36.

35. *Daode jing,* chaps. 37, 48.

36. See Livia Kohn, *Early Chinese Mysticism: Philosophy and Soteriology in the Taoist Tradition* (Princeton: Princeton University Press, 1991), and *Taoist Mystical Philosophy: The Scripture of Western Ascension* (Albany: State University of New York Press, 1991).

37. See Wolfgang Kubin, "Der unstete Affe. Zum Problem des Selbst im Konfuzianismus," in *Konfuzianismus und die Modernisierung Chinas,* ed. Silke Krieger and Rolf Trauzettel (Mainz: Hase und Köhler, 1990), pp. 80–113.

38. Rolf Trauzettel, "Individuum und Heteronomie: Historische Aspekte des Verhältnisses von Individuum und Gesellschaft in China," *Saeculum* 28, no. 3 (1977): 340–64. On the question of how this phenomenon has affected the very fundamental way of thinking of the Chinese, see Rolf Trauzettel, "Denken die Chinesen anders? Komparatistische Thesen zur chinesischen Philosophiegeschichte," in *Anlage zum Mitteilungsblatt* no. 5 (Köln: Deutsche China Gesellschaft, 1988), pp. 1–13.

39. Wolfgang Bauer, "Icherleben und Autobiographie im älteren China," in *Heidelberger Jahrbücher* 8 (1964), 12–40; "Die Eigenanalyse eines Unbekannten: Ichstruktur und Lebensphilosophie in Wang Chiehs (1609–ca. 1680) 'Ausführlicher Selbstdarstellung des Schmarotzers Drei-Ich'," in *Religion und Philosophie in Ostasien: Festschrift für Hans Steininger,* ed. Gert Naundorf, Karl-Heinz Pohl, and Hans Hermann Schmidt (Würzburg: Königshausen and Neumann, 1985), pp. 377–400.

40. See Joseph S. M. Lau, "Duty, Reputation, and Selfhood in Traditional Chinese Narratives," in *Expressions of Self in Chinese Literature,* ed. Robert E. Hegel (New York: Columbia University Press, 1985), pp. 363–83.

41. Ibid., p. 381.

42. See Robert E. Hegel, "An Exploration of the Chinese Literary Self," in Hegel, *Expressions of Self,* pp. 12–13.

43. See Trauzettel, "Individuum und Heteronomie," pp. 347–50.

44. *Analects* 4.5.

45. William Theodore de Bary, "Neo-Confucian Individualism and Holism," in Munro, *Individualism and Holism,* p. 332.

46. *Analects* 4.5. See Tu Wei-ming, "The Confucian Perception of Adulthood," in *Adulthood,* ed. Erik Erikson (New York: W. W. Norton, 1985), pp. 113–20.

47. *Mencius* 4B.12.

48. William Theodore de Bary, *The Liberal Tradition in China* (New York: Columbia University Press, 1983), p. 61.

49. Fingarette, "The Problem of the Self," p. 135.

50. *Nanhua zhenjing zhushu,* ed. *Daozang* fasc. 107–19, pp. 6.15b–16a.

PART III

Selfhood in Theology, Biology, Psychoanalysis, and Politics

Selfhood in the Image of God

KRISTER STENDAHL

IN JEWISH, CHRISTIAN, AND MUSLIM dialogue, especially in relation to the trauma of the Middle East, Christians, Jews, and Muslims all hark back to the understanding of human beings as all created in the image of God. All the other things, however important in defining identity — covenants galore — are secondary.

There is a common yearning and searching back to this part of our traditions: human beings are defined by being created in the image of God. And I find that moving, especially if you give it that colorful rabbinic form as does the question in the Jewish tradition, "Why is it that humanity emerges out of one couple?" Answer: "So that nobody can say that my parents are better than your parents."

So when I thought about selfhood I wanted to speak about the image of God. I had also started to reflect, while writing a booklet for the World Council of Churches in preparation for its next Assembly, on the theme "Come, Holy Spirit, renew the whole creation." And I started to wonder. Being a good Christian theologian, I had learned in my studies that humanity was a beautiful thing in the Bible, that human beings were created in the likeness and image of God. But why was it that this powerful expression of common humanity was really not operative and was rather seldom referred to in the theology and the sermons that had nurtured me? Perhaps because seeking a common identity in our humanity is not distinct enough. It's no fun to work for a company — and I speak especially about the clergy — whose product cannot claim to be unique over against other products.

Even in the Western tradition, where the tone is set by Western Christianity, however attenuated, we have all learned that human beings are created in the image of God — and hence that

141

we could seek our identity and find our place and get our inspiration from that fantastic idea.

But then there is chapter 3 of Genesis, the story of "the Fall." It has been read, especially in the West and by the help of Augustine, so as to be the virtual cancellation of the operative idea of humanity being in the image of God. It is a strange and even teasing story where the woman is active and the man is passive. It's a story in which Adam is approached and asked, "Why do you have those funny clothes on you?" And Adam says, "It wasn't I; it was she," blaming the victim from day one. In the story we do not find words like *Fall* and *sin*, but in Western Christendom it was read with the result that "the image of God" was only the glorious and wonderful background which made the Fall more calamitous.

Elaine Pagels has shown in her wonderful book *Adam, Eve, and the Serpent* that early Christian tradition did not read the story that way. One rather read it as the story about how human beings had moved from innocence to responsibility — or, as it says in biblical language, how they had learned to distinguish between good and evil, thereby being responsible. They were no longer blessed zombies but responsible persons with free will. The story is about responsibility and free will and humankind's risky move from innocence to conscious responsibility. That's how one read it — in a world which often considered human beings as pawns in a game of fate. And in Jesus Christ there was new power to stand up boldly and with human dignity before the authorities, as the martyrs did. That perception of the human condition, which lasted for three hundred years of Christian interpretation, was turned around in the West by Augustine who, according to Pagels, understood human beings as being badly in need of discipline, guidance, and moral reform. Thus much of the dignity of human beings and their conscience and free will was brushed aside. There wasn't very much left of the image of God in the Western Christian person.

Hence that glorious idea was not operative and has been underdeveloped or underused in our Western tradition ever since. I want to go back to those verses in Genesis where it says, "Then God said, let us make Ha-Adam (humanity, the human) in our image after our likeness. Let them (yes, it is plural) have dominion over. . . . So God created Ha-Adam in God's own image. In the image of God, God created Ha-Adam; male and female, God created them" (Gen. 1:26–27). The author cannot really decide whether to use singular or plural, because the author does not know how to handle this problem that human beings are created in the image of God — male and female as they are! Also, this bold play with images appears in a Scripture and a tradition dead set against images of God, making it all the more surprising to speak about humankind being in the image of God.

Here it is worth remembering that human beings did not get a day unto themselves in the Genesis story of creation. If you ask people what was created on what day, people generally think that on the sixth day human beings were created. But we had to share that last work day with all the creeping things and all the walking things. It's almost as if God were musing and said, "Sooner or later, perhaps when Darwin comes, perhaps when they start to listen to the native Americans, they will learn that they are in a binding continuity with the whole creation."

To be created in the image of God is a definition of the self. In Greek this *imago*, this *ikon*, came to be referred to as the *doxa*, the "glory." Paul says that we fall short of the glory of God (Rom. 3:23; cf. Rom. 8:18,21). That is a starting point, and we could say that, as the Bible tells it, God's whole history from Genesis to Revelation is toward the mending, the healing, the restoration of the image of God (2 Cor. 3:18). The image of God is the way to speak about human beings as inviolable. We speak about human rights in our politics, but the inviolable and sacred nature of humanity in the West is rooted in this idea of the *imago dei*, the image of God.

What then about God, the divine self, *the* selfhood? In classical, and especially in Eastern Christian, theology, an understanding of selfhood is not so much found in our relationship to God as it is in reflection on the divine self, God's self. God's selfhood became an object of fascinated reflection in the notion of the Trinity. Christians little by little developed this strange idea. When you ask a person what it is to be a Christian, here in the West people would usually say a Christian is somebody who believes in Jesus Christ. One is a Christian by one's relation to Jesus Christ. But Eastern Christians would say that that is a heresy. One is a Christian when one worships and acknowledges the holy Trinity. *That* is Christian faith.

This trinitarian understanding of God's selfhood was engendered during the first Christian centuries. Only biblicists try to push it back into the Bible. There is often a genetic fallacy in religious circles and in the study of religion, that is, a habit to think that if you know the beginning of something, you know the real thing, the essence. Development is then regarded as decadence. Hence the biblicists have to find the Trinity in the Bible, and liberals are afraid of doctrinal creativity.

To many Christians in the West, it seems strange to think of God as somehow threesome and yet one. And there are jokes about this, and missionary anecdotes about the misunderstandings of the Trinity. People find it hard to believe that it could be important, or they leave it to the theologians because they feel it is without relevance for daily faith and life. But I have come to see that my faith badly needs to be challenged by the Trinity, by the mystery which rescues me from picturing God in all-too-human form. I would like to argue that no earlier period of the Church has pictured God more as a human father figure and Jesus as a man than has the last one hundred and fifty years or so — and at some cost, and with increased gender problems, for this male image of God became oppressive to many women and by implication also to men. What a liberation to be reminded that it is equally true to speak of God as Spirit (and in Greek the Spirit is "it," not "he"). As the theology of the Church was articulated and written by men, this nongendered character of the Spirit was lost by assimilation within the masculine God language. Such an assimilation strikes many as inevitable, especially when the Latin term *persona*, with its original connotations of "actor's mask" or "role," came to translate what the Greeks called *hypostasis*, by which they expressed the concrete, substantive actualizations of divine essence. But *person* spoke more directly to our need for a personal relation to God. So we created God in our own image. And if the Spirit is "a person," then it seemed to require the personal pronoun — either "he" or "she." In the Church, of course, it turned out to be "he," although in Hebrew the Spirit was "she," as was her sister Wisdom (Sophia) in both Hebrew and Greek.

The worship of the triune God is a liberation from that idolatry in which we picture God in our own image. To be sure, we can pray to God in the most intimate personal terms, but when we do, we must avoid the danger of letting our images of God harden into idols with our own racial and gender traits.

So we learn — and this is the mystery of the Trinity — to image God beyond our imagining. This mystery is not in the image of splendid isolation, but eternal being in mutual interrelationships, organic, cosmic, life-giving energy, creative and transcendent. That is strange language. But try to imagine a picture of God that emerged out of these reflections in the East: God not as a self-sufficient entity, but God as total interdependence. There is constant interplay between the Father and the Son and the Spirit, between the Creator, the Redeemer, and the Energy. To think of God as a constant interdependence is not unlike the way post-Newtonian science has learned to think about reality.

That kind of thinking on a deeper level is our perception of the selfhood of God, not as a rarefied entity or even a person. The selfhood of God is an ever-ongoing relationship between the Father and the Son and the Spirit, so that one does not dominate the others. This is not a hierarchy, but a giving and receiving in complete mutuality. There is a famous controversy in the history of Christian theology called the *filioque* controversy. In the East one said that one believed in "the Spirit, the Lord and Giver of Life, who proceeds from the Father." But the West didn't like that because it didn't mention the Son. They always were afraid that if one didn't mention Christ, one wouldn't be a Christian. So with the political support of Charlemagne, the West amended the creed of the Greeks to read: ". . . who proceeds from the Father *and the Son (filioque).*" We Westerners have to have a clear succession line, but how I appreciate the Eastern alternative of pliable interplay, thinking of God as interdependence, thinking in organic language.

There are three languages of biblical and Christian theology, three distinct symbol systems. There is juridical language: God is the judge, and how are human beings to measure up? What can satisfy God's righteousness, and by what sacrifice? Sin and forgiveness and judgment become the axis on which everything happens. That's the Western main line, dominant in Catholicism and Lutheranism. Second, there is the basically Jewish and Calvinist language which is political-social: "Lord," "slave/servant." It is a sociopolitical obedience model, elaborated with numerous covenants. There is a third one which has especially been cultivated by the East, and that is the biological language where the issue is Life. It's a Johannine language: "I have come that they may have life, and have it abundantly" (John 10:10). Here everything is turned toward the furthering of life. The sacraments become the medicine of immortality; sin becomes the obstacle to the free flow of the life blood of God's energy through the system; and evil becomes cancerous. Such language fits well with thinking about God in organic interdependent terms. To learn that grammar one should meditate over the words of Jesus' prayer in the Gospel of John: "I pray . . . that they may all be one; even as thou, Father, art in me and I in thee, that they may also be in us . . . I in them and thou in me. . . ." (John 17:20ff). All these three languages are needed; but as with Paul's famous words about faith, hope, and love, the greatest of the three may be the third.

What then about the human self — our selfhood? If we are created in the image of God, then our being, our selfhood, the essence of being human, is interdependence, giving and receiving in constant mutuality. Giving and receiving become so interdependent that they become simultaneous. This is like the art of lovemaking at its best, when the giving and receiving are indistinguishable from one another. The human self, the selfhood in the image of the triune God, is a marvelous model to meditate upon. This recognized interdependence makes the other necessary for our fulfillment. We live in a time which is very hungry for self-fulfillment, yet much of the Christian tradition speaks about self-denial rather than self-fulfillment. And that self-denial partly comes from the fact that the people who write and do theology are privileged; therefore they speak to themselves about the necessity of control and self-denial. But there are people who don't need to be reminded of self-denial because those in power have taken away from them everything that they could possibly deny themselves. They are the oppressed and the suppressed. And for them the issue is not self-denial, but self-fulfillment.

Being created in the image of God is to be in the image of One whose selfhood is in giving and receiving, who is yearning toward the other, creating a world of others in order to be in relation to them. This recognized interdependence model makes the other necessary for my fulfillment. It is that which is different from me that can add to my life. It is that which is different that carries the promise of renewal.

When I was young, I was taught that "like children make best playmates"—alike in terms of class, race, and so forth. But that is not true. It's boring, especially when compared with the vision of human relationship that the apostle Paul hits upon when he reflects theologically on the diversity of the Christians in Corinth (1 Cor. 13). The key word is love.

Here I must take issue with a countryman and fellow bishop in the Church of Sweden, Anders Nygren, in whose influential book on *Agape and Eros* we are given a caricature of the proper Christian understanding of love. Nygren's God seems to say to us: "My love is so great that I can love a miserable wretch like you." But that is not love; that is condescension. That does not lift anyone up. That is a theological *tour de force*, maximizing the contrast between God and humanity and denying the *imago dei*, the image of God. It's a one-way-traffic love and it does not match even a sound linguistic understanding of the meaning of the Greek word *agape*. It was actually the Jewish translators of the Hebrew Bible who chose this from the many words that the Greek language has for love. They felt that when they read, "Thou shalt love the Lord thy God with all thy heart and all thy mind. . . ." or "Thou shalt love thy neighbor as thyself," the right Greek word was that one, for it has the connotation of esteem, value. Nygren's concept certainly does not have esteem in it. On the contrary, it has condescension. But as I read the Christian texts, I find that Jesus loved sinners because he really liked them. He found something lovable in the sinner, where others did not. And Paul uses this same esteem in dealing with that contentious church in Corinth, making its diversity an asset instead of a liability. And he comes up with the same idea: the recognized interdependence in which you are fulfilled by the other. Therefore he says about love that it does not seek its own. That doesn't mean "it is not selfish." It means that it longs not for the like, but for the unlike; it is insatiable for enrichment in ever giving and receiving. Or as Paul says earlier: "Knowledge puffs up; love builds up" (1 Cor. 8:1).

This seems an odd way of arguing; that somehow the image of God informs the image of our selfhood. Is it not obviously the other way around? Are not our thoughts of God constructions and projections of our selfhood onto God? Perhaps there is more interplay and mutuality even here than we usually allow for. But this I know: when I speak of, when I meditate upon, when I perceive God as that insatiable, dynamic interrelationship, I find always that there is something in God as a mystery which is beyond the sum total of my little images. I glimpse much dignity and wisdom in understanding human selfhood in the image of God, and that glimpse is liberating. This interdependent God, with whom I am interdependent, is One "whom to serve is perfect freedom."

The Organismal Self in Its Philosophical Context

ALFRED I. TAUBER

I. PROVISOS, CAVEATS, AND OTHER MISGIVINGS

ONE MIGHT EXPECT the biosciences to offer some crucial insight into defining the self. The lessons learned in a system governed by rigorous proof and refutation might give certain credence to one point of view or another. But this is the basis of the terribly misplaced "lessons" applied by the Nazis and Lysenko, and in our time by biosociologists and creationists, in their various causes. We must be wary of misapplied or misconstrued theory, so my first concern is to resist and disavow allegiance to any sociopolitical program. At the same time, I will argue that there is a biological offering to our understanding of selfhood, and that it is embedded in a metaphysical foundation that underlies a broad cultural experience. I will explore the elusive relationship between that scientific construction and its wider intellectual milieu. Perhaps biology even offers a unique mirror of that milieu. But which biology?

There are divergent philosophical attitudes, often hidden, which serve as intellectual forces in creating the operative scientific paradigm. Thus competing visions of modern biology generate various ideas of the self. I deliberately choose an organismally based biology, so I must warn the reader that there are numerous and varied biomedical definitions of the self, depending on the individual's parochial prism of assumptions, interests, methodologies, history, and language. But for the various bioscientists, each proffering the distinctive voice of her discipline, the problem of the self rests at the fulcrum of her interest and serves as the metaphysical boundary of her orientation. By discerning that image, we gain insight into how we regard the elusive self.

Certain biological disciplines, however, disdain employing the *self* as a useful term. For some, it immediately connotes anthropocentricity, which in turn implies self-consciousness. It is the term of a completed and a bounded entity. *Organism* is generally the preferred term. For instance, the evolutionist debates whether the focus of selection is the organism or another organizational level; the microbiologist might consider individual bacteria as only a component of a larger organizational conglomerate; the developmental biologist might debate the basis of identity that governs the maturation of the embryo. *Self* in these contexts serves to define distinctness, biological unity, organismal identity.[1] As such, selfhood seeks approbation as just one of the several qualities that describe life. To me, however, selfhood is more fundamental.

In the simplest sense, the self is the genetic complement of the organism. The DNA code offers the potential of development, interaction with the environment, and reproduction. But to leave the self at this level, claiming only rudiments of identity as a particular allotment of DNA, is to deny the entire spectrum of the life process as just so much fuss to preserve and pass on that encapsulated genetic morsel. Arguing a hegemonic claim for the essentiality of DNA is to adhere to a restricted vision of biology. One enthusiast announces:

> It is raining DNA outside. . . . The cotton wool is made mostly of cellulose, and it dwarfs the capsule that contains DNA, the genetic information. The DNA content must be a small proportion of the total so why did I say that it was raining DNA rather than raining cellulose? The answer is that it is the DNA that matters. . . . The whole performance — cotton wool, catkins, tree, and all — is in aid of one thing and one thing only, the spreading of DNA around the countryside.[2]

We intuit however that this is a distortion. Nature must encompass interactive selves, entities with identities. Genetics offers a definition of the self, but molecular biology does so only as one of many aspects of its endeavor.

In fact, the self demands its own disciplines to deal with the varied interactions with its environment and within itself. If we seek a science that addresses the nature of the self, neuroscience and immunology offer more comprehensive definitions. Each shares fundamental similarities: they employ perceptive mechanisms, cognitive processing, and effector mechanisms. The self as the object of their enquiry becomes the focus of a particular question of biology. What confers identity as an interactive, dynamic, challenged entity? The DNA offers the blueprint of action but the organismal self does the living. Controversy over the primacy of each approach dates to the 1840s, when German physiologists deliberately purged vitalism from biology. They provided an important service, but their program of reductionism, to seek the physico-chemical basis of life by identifying the most basic elements of physiology and inheritance, led to the radical reductionism of our own time. That history serves as a disapproving witness and countervailing theme of this discussion. Selfhood based on organismal biology takes on a very different flavor than that recognized by those who view our science with an exclusively reductive bent.

II. THE IMMUNE SELF

In 1884, Elie Metchnikoff proposed a revolutionary notion of the organism.[3] The subsequent history of his idea has proven powerful and will serve as the basis of our biological perspective on the self. He was an embryologist who began his career shortly after Darwin published the *Origin of Species* (1859). He was thus engaged in the ensuing debate over how physiological or developmental mechanisms were driven by evolutionary forces. Metchnikoff was interested in defining the evolutionary fate of one of the three primordial embryonic layers from which adult structures emerged. Of these, the middle layer (the mesoderm) was highly problematic as to its origin and relation to the other layers. The mesoderm has mobile, engulfing cells, which Metchnikoff studied as markers of mesodermal activity in the various stages of development.

These cells had been recognized for several decades, but Metchnikoff made a remarkable discovery. They possess diverse functions that are determined by the different stages of the organism. In embryo, for example, the engulfing (phagocyte) cells serve to remodel tissue, acting as an architectural agent of construction. For instance, the tail of the tadpole is devoured by these phagocytes prior to the emergence of the mature frog. This "eating" function simply reflects preserved activity observed in primitive animals where these cells serve as the nutrient organ to capture food and feed its compatriots. In organisms with an intestine the phagocyte no longer acts as the food gatherer. It retains, however, its primitive function of eating, but now to act as the purveyor of the organism's identity and integrity. First, the phagocyte defines what is to be destroyed or preserved. Effete, damaged, malignant, senile cells are to be removed. Identity is thus established as the phagocyte directs its activities against itself. The same police action is taken against the foreign, the intruder. In this vector of other-directedness, the phagocyte defends the organism, and thus preserves organismal integrity. Pathologists' interest in Metchnikoff's hypothesis, as well as his own research efforts, were addressed to this latter function as the nascent field of microbiology sought to elucidate host-parasite interactions. Immunology as a distinct discipline grew from these beginnings.

Metchnikoff revolutionized biology by asserting that immunity was an active process. More profoundly, he viewed integrity not as a given, but as an attainment in an unceasing process of self-definition. The challenge of an ever-changing environment is the external context of an organism's self-preservation, but Metchnikoff regarded the organism's very identity as also requiring self-renewal, identification, and self-definition. Selfhood is under constant assault, and the phagocyte is the mediator of the process that defines host integrity, a process directed both against the environment and inward, as the organism changes in time.

Metchnikoff's theory was viewed as both teleological and vitalistic, in the sense that what determines selfhood is simply the striving of phagocytes for their aggrandizement. Their activity, competing with other cell lines, is Darwin's struggle of species turned inward within the organism. Here then is a profoundly novel concept of health. No longer are the ancient humors in balance, but life's cellular components are in conflict. Health is not given; it is achieved. The potential disharmonious assembly of evolved constituents must now strive for harmony. For Metchnikoff, this was a purposeful process, one not given but attained in conflict and actively achieved. He was severely monistic, not on an axis of normal to pathological, but saw self-actualization as mediated by an essentially pathological process, the expression of a subsystem (that is, phagocytes serving as immune cells) defining the normative. The norm thus arises from evolutionary necessity.

It is at the interface of physiology (the present) and evolution (the historical) that a conceptual integration must be made. Metchnikoff endeavored to harness his immune concepts to establish the ideal norm and annul disease. But the derivative function of his thinking places him outside the thrust of orthodox nineteenth-century conceptions concerning the nature of pathology and its dynamic role in defining health. Metchnikoff *began* with disharmony. Health then is actively sought; restoration of health implies an initial harmony; but for him this state remains an ever-elusive ideal. He clearly falls closest to dynamic models, but the orientation is completely reversed from other nineteenth-century biologists. For example, immunity prior to the phagocytosis theory was a passive concept. As late as 1880, Louis Pasteur thought second infections were prevented because of exhaustion of critical nutrients during initial infections. As in a test tube, when the bacteria consumed their growth factors, a stable plateau ensued, followed by death. When immunity was demonstrated with dead organisms, Metchnikoff's position took on a new legitimacy.

Physiology offers another clear example of Metchnikoff's novelty. Claude Bernard's concept of homeostasis is very different from that held by Metchnikoff. Both agreed on the organism's striving for health, but their respective vectors were reversed. Bernard assumed an idealized physiology — quantitatively and qualitatively. Metchnikoff allowed no such initial harmony, for as an evolutionist, he regarded the organism as forever striving for perfection.

The extension of the normal to the pathological, along a continuum, became the formalized problem for nineteenth-century pathology.[4] Various schools converged on the central concept that the abnormal followed the same laws as the normal, and the phenomena of disease differed from health only in terms of intensity. But for Metchnikoff health was never the norm, only the idealized goal. Pathology then became potentially restorative. "Physiological inflammation" was his code for that curative process. Disharmony was the norm, and harmonization the ideal. The consequences of that vector of thought generated the idea of active host defense, definition of selfhood, active organismal integrity, and establishment of harmony as an ideal process to eventuate in health.[5] Immunity was the means of defining selfhood, and this formed the essence of homeostasis.

Metchnikoff's conception of organism and health largely remained an unrecognized, but implicit, pillar of immunology.[6] The traces of his metaphysics lay buried in the intellectual origin of modern medicine and have emerged only recently. The fate of the phagocytosis theory is complex and involuted. Metchnikoff was awarded the Nobel Prize in 1908, but his broad vision of the self was not appreciated at the time. Only after World War II did biology again reexamine immune mechanisms beyond those offering protection to the organism's integrity. They now explored how immunity defined the organism, both as a self and as an identity in the context of the Other. The problems of autoimmunity and transplantation biology now focus upon such questions of identity, and the general concerns of self-definition as an active process. Metchnikoff's concepts are of immense heuristic value in answering these questions.

The immune system as a cognitive apparatus invests the organism with a purposeful mechanism analogous to the neurologic system, where perceptions are processed and action taken to fulfill goals of nourishment, reproduction, protection, and so forth. The Metchnikovian insight was to apply such active behavior to the inner workings that define the organism and maintain its integrity. The fundamental basis of Metchnikoff's thinking rested on the indeterminate nature of organismal integrity, which was attained only by an ongoing process of self-definition. The self was no longer clearly delineated as a given entity. The "boundaries" of the organism were constantly reestablished under the assault of temporal change and environmental challenge. A contrasting pictorial image would be the Cubist or Fauvist vision of the object fusing to its contextual surroundings, and thus blurred in its identity. But that challenge remained and was resisted by an ethos that fundamentally asserted the organism's active striving for self-definition. This scientific context assumes a most intriguing philosophical position, one central to the concerns of the period.

III. THE QUESTION OF THE *ZEITGEIST*

Metchnikoff's metaphysical vision of the organism had few adherents in his research community.[7] To the extent his ideas were addressed, the dialogue was conducted in a language of a restricted grammar, that is, immunochemical identification of various immune reactions. The dynamic biology of the phagocyte as he formulated it was not a serious research topic for investigation. But had Metchnikoff wished to discuss the full implications of his theory, he would have found sympathetic listeners among philosophers and artists of the period. What appears to be a revolutionary concept in biology, seeming to arise *de novo* from Darwinian problems, in fact is found throughout the humanities as a response to the pessimism and nihilism of the period.

Metchnikoff's formulation is grounded in his concept of the disharmonious organism that requires a subsystem to take control of harmonizing disparate, competing centers of activity. This vision reflected his own psychology. During early adulthood he was afflicted with several severe depressive episodes, marked by a global pessimism and punctuated by at least two suicide attempts.[8] One of the most remarkable aspects of the genesis of the phagocytosis theory is that it emerged during the psychological resolution of his personal difficulties.

Metchnikoff's psychohistory sheds fascinating insight on how he thought in the seemingly objective world of embryology. This scenario is not unique and is echoed by two philosophers of the period: Friedrich Nietzsche and William James. Each faced similar nihilistic challenges and each responded intellectually in similar fashion to Metchnikoff. James was born in 1842, Nietzsche in 1844, Metchnikoff in 1845. Each suffered from episodic incapacitating psychosomatic depressive illness: James most severely in 1869–72, Nietzsche in 1876–79, and Metchnikoff in 1873 and 1880, when he attempted suicide. Each dealt with his pessimism with a philosophical response in antithesis to Schopenhauer, who exerted profound influence on each man during his early twenties. Beyond these interesting biographical notes, we have strong evidence that their respective philosophies closely followed their psychological state.[9] But did their respective trials and intellectual resolution of an emotional predicament reflect a broader cultural ethos?

The literature of such relationships is immense, but superficially there is an abundance of cultural heroes representing a similar pattern. Countervailing the nihilism and decadence of the period are such heroes as Teddy Roosevelt, who mythologized his strength of character by overcoming physical infirmity; Horatio Alger's rags-to-riches heroes who overcame economic deprivation, and thus attested to the power of resolute self-reliance; Kipling's affirmation of imperialistic ideals as resting on the strength of devoted subjects; Gauguin's creation of a personal primitive mythology to redefine his artistic being. The list could go on and on, but our image of the period might just as easily conjure the effete, the decadent, the fatalistic, for the nineteenth century failed to resolve the complex romantic split of the self in its heroic, if tragic, struggle with fate and psyche. I can make no attempt even to outline such complex issues, but will attempt to validate Metchnikoff's formulation of selfhood by illustrating what appear to be parallel constructions by James and Nietzsche, as key philosophical architects of this period. The coincidences of age and experience only highlight how they might be regarded as kindred spirits at some fundamental level, where their respective thought complements a similar vision of the self.

IV. RADICAL EMPIRICISM

William James's radical empiricism defines consciousness as a "selecting agency," "the very hull on which our mental ship is built," forming the "nucleus of our inner self."[10] This is the central motif of *The Principles of Psychology*, the magnum opus begun in 1878 and published in 1890. It views the mind as an active, selective self, whose volition is dictated by attention: "Each of us literally *chooses*, by his ways of attending to things, what sort of a universe he shall appear to himself to inhabit."[11]

Human action — volition, thought, reorganization and manipulation of the environment — arises from the Darwinian position that individual variation constitutes the basis for adaptive change and adjustment, and in that context the individual senses freedom of action and the unique value of the individual. The world must then be organized from "one great blooming, buzzing confusion"[12] by selecting both objects of attentions and interests. Attention is regarded as voluntary, not merely a response to external stimuli. In the same year Metchnikoff published his first phagocytosis studies (1884), James wrote "On Some Omissions of Introspective Psychology," (the basis of Chapter 9 of *Principles*). There he attacked the Humean sense data epistemology, disallowing a simple empiricism, and argued that there were no simple sensations, but "results of discriminative attention, pushed to a very high degree."[13] The Lockean combination of "simple ideas" has no true permanence. Only active sorting and combining makes it possible to experience an object. We process sensations as "stepping stones to pass over to the recognition for the realities whose presence they reveal."[14]

At the same time, painters such as Monet and Seurat were demonstrating the enormous complexity of visual perception, where highly variegated color was coalesced and processed as an image with certain uniformity and finiteness. Absolute quantities or qualities were replaced with synthesized ratios and conglomerates. The radical orientation of this period in large measure rests upon the *self-consciousness* of such processing, for Goethe was already concerned in the 1790s with the construction of scientific facts in the concept of accepted theory.

> It is easy to see the risk we run when we try to connect a single bit of evidence with an idea already formed. . . . Such efforts generally give rise to theories and systems which are a tribute to their author's intelligence [but may] harm the very progress of the human mind they had earlier assisted.[15]

And Rushkin by mid-century was acknowledging the role of attention in perception and aesthetics:

> The mind vacant of knowledge and destitute of sensibility, and the external object becomes little more to us than it is to birds or insects. . . . On the other hand, let the reasoning powers be shrewd in excess, the knowledge vast, or sensibility intense . . . the object will suggest so much that it shall be soon itself forgotten, or become at the utmost, merely a kind of key note to the course of purposeful thought.[16]

But James was to carry what Goethe called the old truth and what Rushkin called *sight* to a formalized philosophy.

The experiencing mind, that is, one adaptive along the dimension of time, where experience remolds us and objects of inquiry are never viewed in the same context or from the same perspective, demands a dynamic organizational psychology. An atomistic view of an unchanging world simply will not support James's psychology. And thus beyond the active component of his system, the parallel to Metchnikoff resides in the holistic nature of thinking, where the Jamesian self acts in its full phenomenological context.

James's most consistent, and probably most lasting, contribution was his insistence on a phenomenal totality.[17] "Thought suffused with the consciousness of all that dim context"[18] refers to all that structures our experience, and which can only be analyzed reflectively. Our selection and ordering of experience is present in every perception, and in fact we "ignore most of the things before us."[19] Thinking thus involves choice, and what interests us are those objects of practical or aesthetic importance. He seems to have concluded that the need for selectivity of consciousness is an ever-changing flux of reality won by arbitrarily arresting experience. Conceptualization requires isolating and distinguishing some aspects, excluding others, and ordering reality not by hard and fast divisions, but by personal processing. Experience then enters not as bare or raw data, but according to the needs of the one experiencing. Experience is thus manipulated to serve our needs, and the self is invested as an inviolate *me*, and a self-defining, unique individual:

> Even the trodden worm . . . contrasts his own suffering self with the whole remaining universe, though he have no clear conception either of himself or what the universe may be. He is for me a mere part of the world; for him it is I who am the mere part. Each of us dichotomizes the cosmos in a different place.[20]

This is not the forum to evaluate Jamesian consciousness beyond noting that he struggled throughout his career to recount how we share a common world, to reconcile the individual's experience as consistent with a common universe.[21] At some points he assumed a primordial experience;[22] at others, a resignation to the irrational connectedness of nature, the consistency of experience responsive to our subjective purposes as "a miracle not yet exhaustively cleared up by any philosophy."[23] Essentially James defaulted in postulating how mind functioned, having "grown up in ways of which at present we can give no account."[24] Ultimately the nature of the experienced self is left an open question, remaining as a description of interactive processes of that self with the world. His later doubts concerning the role of rationalism still leave an active self to order and experience the world, for as he wrote in *Varieties of Religious Experience*, nature is "a vast *plenum* in which our attention draws capricious lines in innumerable directions."[25] I will not attempt to further characterize James's evolved position. Whether we regard him as a pre-Husserlian phenomenologist, an antiphenomenologist, a precursor of Whiteheadian process philosophy, or a modern hermeneutist, I wish only to focus upon his forcefully energetic engagement with the environment, where the self actively selects and constructs its world from the bewildering complexity of the surrounding plenum. The self must thereby differentiate itself, and it does so only by active engagement. The Metchnikovian self is vividly reiterated in this epistemology.

V. NIHILISM AND THE SELF

Although the centrality of action and the activity of willing may be traced back to Kant and Leibniz, and the self's function in creating its object — for example, moral (Fichte) and aesthetic (Schelling) — preoccupied Romantic philosophers, Friedrich Nietzsche is the consummate metaphysician of the active self, and more profoundly, the self constantly striving for self-definition in an evolutionary process. The elusiveness of Nietzsche's thought may be unified as a theory of individuality. Despite the absence of general formulas, Nietzsche posits a striving hero, reflecting active and self-conscious growth into himself, and what emerges is a modern Prometheus. The noble goal of perfectionism is crucial, but more fundamental is the struggle itself, for the actuating force is the will to struggle.

> The wretched spiritual game of goals and intentions and motives is only a foreground — even though weak eyes may take them for the matter itself.[26]

The context of the struggle is of course against nihilism, and in the process, a self-created moral universe is sought, never established, always forming. The self is to be actualized in its struggle — in its self-definition of its world as the manifestation of will to power. That energy is directed against nihilism, a false world with decadent values that negates the self as actualizer. The energy source of will, and the final arbiter of value, is the self. And here we must reach into two different dimensions to seek a composite understanding.

The first is Nietzsche's epistemology, which closely relates him to James. There is a fundamental skepticism that pervades Nietzsche's thought, leading to his well-known critique of morality, but beginning with how he defines subject-object relations.[27] Nietzsche uses the image of a man standing with his back toward a supposed reality and the mirror of his mind before him; the perceiver himself blocks an unobstructed view of the world. The thing-in-itself is then only an abstraction, imagined in a world where the perceiver is absent, and approximated at a point beyond the multiple perceptions attained as the subject steps about to obtain mirrored views from various angles. Human beings can know the world only as they measure, perceive, and interpret it. Nietzsche's skepticism is profound, reaching into the mind ("The human intellect cannot avoid seeing itself in its own perspectives and *only* in these")[28] and its object, the world:

> There is absolutely no escape, no back way or bypath into the *real world!* We sit within our net, we spiders, and whatever we catch in it, we catch nothing at all except that which allows itself to be caught in precisely *our* net.[29]

This perspectivism is similar to James's radical epistemology, with all of its limitations of defining a common cosmos and connections between perceivers. But each philosophy allows the individual to become the ultimate interpreter of his world.

Nietzsche's epistemology then leads to his metaphysics. Again, using the technique of the mirror, he argues, "One loves ultimately one's desires, not the thing desired."[30] The true object is the self: "In the final analysis, one experiences only oneself,"[31] but it is a self of multidimensionality, constantly changing, perceiving, and feeling from multiple perspectives. The self is thus conceived as a pluralistic construction. Perspectivism yields a dynamic, responsive, ever-changing self — unfolded, discovered, peeled like an onion, but never completely discovered or defined.[32] The self, like its object, is elusive and always developing, or as Zarathustra proclaimed, "Become what you are." It is in this context that Zarathustra's famous pronouncement, "God is Dead," must be explored.

If we follow a dialogical formula of human relation to the deity, self-definition is found in the encounter. If radical self-directed encounter defines the subject's other, then only the self may define its other. Such a postulate underlies Nietzsche's metaphysics of the will to power. The self is ultimately left inviolate:

> No matter how far a man may extend himself with his knowledge, no matter how objectively he may come to view himself, in the end it can yield to him nothing but his own biography.[33]

VI. WILL TO POWER

Nietzsche, like Metchnikoff, viewed human beings as subject to conflicting instincts and drives. The spectrum of human action results from their internal competition, and thus perspectivism is not only a means of interacting with the world, but is a result of instinctual human conflicts.

> It is our needs that interpret the world; our drives and their For and Against. Every drive is a kind of lust to rule; each one has its perspective that it would like to compel all the other drives to accept as a norm.[34]

Nietzsche, again like Metchnikoff, views human beings as disharmonious, and the ideal resolution of this disharmony serves as the object of human will.

> To become master of the chaos one is; to compel one's chaos to become form: to become logical, simple, unambiguous, mathematics, *law* — that is the grand ambition here.[35]

Heirs of Darwin, both Nietzsche and Metchnikoff viewed the individual as suffering from internal struggle, whose harmonization required a mechanism to resolve conflict. Whether will to power, arising from the self alone and subject to no Other, might serve that function, is the focus of concern.

Nietzsche's mature position corresponds closely to the presentation of Metchnikoff's theory of immunity and the midpoint of James's writing of *Principles*. *Thus Spoke Zarathustra* (composed between 1883 and 1885) and *The Will to Power*, edited selections from his last notebooks (1883–1888), were written during the axial period in which Nietzsche most clearly articulated his reaction to negative nihilism, the most powerful assertion of will and self-construction in modern philosophy.

Martin Heidegger, who unabashedly used Nietzsche for his own designs, offers a highly evocative reading for our purposes. Nietzsche's exploration served as the opening of Heidegger's thought, for both believed that Western philosophy had omitted the essential search for our ontological basis. Their emphasis is not always the same. Corngold notes that "for Heidegger the question is the meaning of Being; for Nietzsche the question is *our* being—the self."[36] However, in the final analysis, after much philosophical juggling, "The 'answer' to the question, what is the self? is the anonymous language of the very question."[37] We are ultimately left with the self as a generative concept, for when Nietzsche asks what created will, Zarathustra responds, "the creative self."[38] Here we find the Heideggerian Nietzsche, in the form of *Dasein*, the self that inquires of Being and finds it as "will."

Heidegger interprets Nietzsche's will to power as no less than "will to will, which is to say, willing is self-willing."[39] The will is more fundamental than a cause or manifestation or psyche—it is the bedrock characterizing Being itself. Will is not the prosaic organic striving force, nor a Schopenhauerian pure abstraction somehow divorced from its subject. It is the essence of Being, and thus it remains fundamentally elusive and undefined, but ever present and discernible. Will is mastery over something, reaching out beyond itself, as affect, as passion, as command. For Heidegger's Nietzsche, will to power not only constitutes the basic character of all beings; it also underlies his metaphysical thinking. Will is an active process, a becoming, with a self-conscious historicism, as opposed to a being, frozen in time.

This contrast between being and becoming is characteristic of post-Darwinian thinking. Evolution pervaded the very structure of experience generating a profound appreciation of how we live in an ever-changing universe. Such an awareness of time made new demands on how the self regarded its world and its own self-hood. Nietzsche was profoundly affected by this post-Darwinian construction of time and its implications: "To impose upon becoming the character of being — that is the supreme *will to power*."[40] The issue is becoming — all process or individualization, that is, as the self, being actualized by *will*, in *time*. Nietzsche ironically invokes the Metchnikovian image!

> What man wants, what every smallest part of a living organism wants, is an increase of power. . . . Let us take the simplest case, that of primitive nourishment: the protoplasm extends its pseudopodia in search of something that resists it — not from hunger but from will to power. Thereupon it attempts to overcome, appropriate, assimilate what it encounters: what one calls "nourishment" is merely a derivative phenomenon, an application of the original will to become *stronger*.[41]

If Metchnikoff offered a biological formulation of the self, and James an epistemologic definition, then Nietzsche is the metaphysician where self-assertion is always a process of returning into its essence, into the origins, and in the process, becoming. Zarathustra is the prophet proclaiming that all being is will to power and this self-assertion is the basis of erecting the concept of the Overman, the champion of postnihilism. To master oneself requires the greatest power to harness the chaos of life into a continual self-overcoming of life. The assertion of will in its purest expression is Zarathustra's herald: "I am that *which must overcome itself again and again*."[42]

VII. FROM NIHILISM TO THE SELF

I was charged to reflect on the self from the biological perspective. In offering Metchnikoff's theory of immunity, dependent on an active, self-defining organism, I chose to orient his notions in the broadest philosophical context of his day. His vision, truly revolutionary in the biological world, was in fact echoed in different guises by James and Nietzsche. Their affinity for each other, however, may better reflect our perceptions, for there is no presumption that the thought of one man directly influenced another. However, they each posited a self of volition, an active, interpretative, self-aggrandizing entity; never completed and always redefined, this organismal self has ever-changing boundaries of integrity. Identity is thus achieved dynamically and not assumed as given. The task then for each is to create the self: Metchnikoff envisioned the organism striving for harmony amongst competing, disparate elements; James sought to place the individual in its particular context in a plenum of experience by selection and volition; Nietzsche's Zarathustra proclaimed humanity as becoming, striving to overcome, and in the process of re-creation, denying nihilistic destruction. Rimbaud's dissolution of the self ("Je est un autre." [I is someone else.])[43] is firmly rejected. Yet even a century later, their concepts appear to challenge our own deeply felt notions of a given, defined organism and a moral deist-dependent universe.

We seem to have inherited a conflict that may be dated to the *fin-de-siecle*, namely defining an individualistic ethos in a "culture of narcissism" and a deconstructionist mentality. Rimbaud's shadow is still pervasively present. A recent popular song evokes a nostalgic refrain of our persistent need:

> Superman never made any money
> Was saving the world for Mahatma Gandhi
> And sometimes I despair
> The world will never see another man like him.[44]

The Overman became Superman, a dismal cartoon of Nietzsche's vision, but at least he filtered through to the popular mind. Unfortunately he is from another, superhuman world, and beyond our ken — physically and ethically. It is a sorry state, but at least we perceive that the cultural ethos recognizes our predicament — vulgarized and distorted, yet nevertheless discernible in faint outline.

Heidegger also began with a heroic quest. His ontologic search begins with the inquiring *Dasein*, the spirit that seeks, and in examining how *Dasein* searches the boundaries of his existence, he displays the outline of Being. We need not be Heideggerians to discern the profound reaches into our very essence that an active self demands, but it bespeaks a rejection of a nihilism, an assertion of individuality, and a promise of freedom that allures us. The *Zeitgeist* of any period is a selective construction, and if we see such an outline in James, Metchnikoff, and Nietzsche, it must ultimately be due to their appeal in reinforcing our own endeavor, vision, and dream.

NOTES

1. Alfred I. Tauber, ed., *Organism and the Origins of Self* (Dordrecht: Kluwer Academic Pubs., 1991).

2. Richard Dawkins, *The Blind Watchmaker* (New York: W. W. Norton & Co., 1986), p. 111.

3. Alfred I. Tauber and Leon Chernyak, *Metchnikoff and the Origins of Immunology: From Metaphor to Theory* (Oxford and New York: Oxford University Press, 1991).

4. George Canguilhem, *The Normal and the Pathological*, trans. C. R. Fawcett (New York: Zone Books, 1989).

5. Alfred I. Tauber, "The Immunological Self: A Centenary Perspective," *Perspectives in Biology and Medicine* 35 (1991): 74–86.

6. Alfred I. Tauber, "The Birth of Immunology 3: The Fate of Phagocytosis Theory," *Cell Immunology* 139 (1992): 505, 530.

7. Ibid.; see also Tauber and Chernyak, *Metchnikoff and the Origins of Immunology*.

8. Olga Metchnikoff, *Life of Elie Metchnikoff*, trans. E. R. Lankester (London: Constable, 1924).

9. Jacques Barzun, *A Stroll with William James* (Chicago: University of Chicago Press, 1983); and Ronald Hayman, *Nietzsche: A Critical Life* (New York: Oxford University Press, 1980).

10. William James, *The Principles of Psychology* (Cambridge: Harvard University Press, 1983), pp. 142, 640, 423.

11. Ibid., p. 401.

12. Ibid., p. 402.

13. Ibid., p. 219.

14. Ibid., p. 225.

15. Johann Wolfgang von Goethe, "The Experiment as Mediator Between Object and Subject," *Scientific Studies* (originally published in 1792), ed. and trans. D. Miller (New York: Suhrkamp Pubs., 1988), pp. 11–17.

16. John Rushkin, *Modern Painters* (London: J. M. Dent, n.d.), p. 270.

17. Charlene H. Seigfried, *William James's Radical Reconstruction of Philosophy* (Albany: State University of New York Press, 1990).

18. James, *Principles of Psychology*, p. 227.

19. Ibid., p. 273.

20. Ibid., p. 278.

21. Seigfried, *William James's Radical Reconstruction of Philosophy*.

22. William James, *Some Problems of Philosophy* (New York: Longmans, Green, & Co., 1931; originally published in 1911).

23. William James, *The Will to Believe* (New York: Longmans, Green, & Co., 1896).

24. James, *Principles of Psychology*, p. 1280.

25. William James, *The Varieties of Religious Experience* (New York: Random House Modern Library, 1902), p. 429.

26. Friedrich Nietzsche, *The Will to Power*, trans. W. Kaufmann and R. J. Hollingdale (New York: Vintage Books, 1967), p. 518.

27. Leslie P. Thiele, *Friedrich Nietzsche and the Politics of the Soul* (Princeton, N.J.: Princeton University Press, 1990).

28. Friedrich Nietzsche, *The Gay Science*, trans. W. Kaufmann (New York: Random House, 1974), p. 336.

29. Friedrich Nietzsche, *Daybreak*, trans. R. J. Hollingdale (Cambridge: At the University Press, 1982), p. 73.

30. Friedrich Nietzsche, *Beyond Good and Evil*, in *The Philosophy of Nietzsche*, trans. H. Zimmern (New York: Random House, 1954), p. 471.

31. Friedrich Nietzsche, *Thus Spoke Zarathustra*, trans. R. J. Hollingdale (New York: Vintage Books, 1967), p. 173.

32. Thiele, *Friedrich Nietzsche and the Politics of the Soul*, p. 215.

33. Friedrich Nietzsche, *Human, All Too Human*, trans. R. J. Hollingdale (Cambridge: At the University Press, 1986).

34. Nietzsche, *Will to Power*, p. 267.

35. Ibid., p. 444.

36. Stanley Corngold, "The Question of the Self in Nietzsche During the Axial Period (1882-1888), in *Why Nietzsche Now?*, ed. D. O'Hara (Bloomington: Indiana University Press, 1985), p. 59.

37. Ibid., p. 67.

38. Nietzsche, *Thus Spoke Zarathustra*, p. 62.

39. Martin Heidegger, *Nietzsche*, trans. D. F. Krell (San Francisco: Harper & Row, 1979), vol. 1.

40. Nietzsche, *Will to Power*, p. 330.

41. Ibid., p. 373.

42. Nietzsche, *Thus Spoke Zarathustra*, p. 138.

43. J. N. A. Rimbaud, *Complete Works: Selected Letters* (Chicago: University of Chicago Press, 1966), p. 305.

44. Crash Test Dummies, "Superman's Song."

Psychoanalysis and the Self:
Toward a Spiritual Point of View

JOHN E. MACK

Not very long ago I had a dream
So bright and glowing it startled me
Into a great glow of transcendental joy.
The dream? Everything around me black as sin
I, walking toward some unknown goal,
My body virginal in youth and pure,
Naked, rosy and quite beautiful.
And from me emanated shining light;
While all about me I could dimly see
Small swarthy men with evil weaponry,
Arms thrust out to mutilate and kill,
Ready to slash through my integrity.
But as they came within my numinosity
They melted into darkness and were gone
And I walked on, untroubled and serene.

> Harriet Robey, aged 90, Freudian trained
> psychiatric social worker, "reared with-
> out belief in God." August, 1991

THE TITLE OF THIS PAPER relates to a 1959 article by David Rapaport and Merton Gill, entitled "The Points of View and Assumptions of Metapsychology."[1] Rapaport and Gill suggested that there are five fundamental points of view which inform psychoanalytic theory and practice and the psychodynamic psychotherapies that derive from psychoanalysis. These are (1) the dynamic point of view, which concerns the direction and magnitude of psychological forces; (2) the economic point of view, which has to do with the

169

distribution and transformation of psychological or emotional ener-
gies; (3) the structural point of view, which describes the more or
less permanent configurations of the psyche, or those which are
slow to change; (4) the genetic point of view, which concerns propo-
sitions about psychological origins and individual development;
and (5) the adaptive point of view, which demands that psychodynamic explanations take into consideration our relationship to
the environment and questions of survival in the external world.
I argue that depth psychology is now in need of a sixth, a spiritual, point of view in order to understand more fully the psyche
and conditions of human life as we now experience them.

The above assumptions are based on too limited a view of
the psyche and have been unable, therefore, to provide a basis for
addressing many of the fundamental problems that we now confront in clinical, social, and political settings. Addictive disorders,
child abuse and other forms of domestic violence, the variety of
complex conditions brought together as personality disorders, the
increased reliance on affect-muting psychotropic drugs and the
turning away of many patients from traditional therapies to "holistic" or "alternative" treatment approaches (which themselves include spiritual elements), reflect profound unmet emotional hun-
gers that psychoanalysts and other mental health professionals are
finding difficult to understand and treat within established theoretical frameworks and therapeutic parameters. Contemporary self
psychology, pioneered by Heinz Kohut and his followers,[2] reflects
this basic dissatisfaction within the field. Psychologist Philip Cushman has applied the term "empty self" to sum up this contemporary sense that something is wrong or missing.[3] At the same time,
out-of-control global crises of human origin, such as the rampant
destruction of the living environment, the spread of ethno-national
violence, and the proliferation of weapons of mass destruction, are
forcing us to reexamine the nature of the psyche or self and our relationship to nature and one another, individually and collectively.

Spiritual matters are by nature subjective and complex. They
are difficult to discuss within a scientific or empirical framework.
But spiritual experience is so fundamental a dimension of the inner lives of human beings throughout the world, and the language
of spirituality so universal a way of speaking, that the task is worth
undertaking.

Spirituality is often associated with dramatic personal events, such as religious conversions,[4] and other peak "highs" or mystical experiences, which we tend to disparage. Yet as Barbara Marx Hubbard has written,

> What sexuality was to the Victorian Age, mystical experience is to ours. Almost everyone experiences it, but almost no one dares to speak about it. We have been dominated by a scientific, materialistic culture which has made us feel embarrassed about our natural spiritual natures. Yet we read that sixty percent of the American people have had mystical experiences. We are a nation of repressed mystics![5]

But most spiritual experiences are less dramatic and more subtle. They have in common the sense that there is another reality beyond that which is immediately manifest to our senses or reason. This reality is numinous, that is, mysterious and containing or filled with a power that is beyond comprehension, called "divine" when it seems to contain something of a wondrous nature or higher value beyond ourselves.

Also fundamental to religious experience and to an apprehension of the divine is the sense that the universe is not simply a chance creation or a random flux of matter and energy, but that there is some sort of design, or even intention. The nature or direction of this intentional design is, however, beyond our knowing. Paradoxically the way to get a little closer to knowing is to acknowledge our not knowing and the depths of mystery it embodies. When a sense of the divine becomes embodied in a single feature or a multiplicity of beings, people speak of God or gods. The spiritual world is also reflected in the myths that native people have created since before the beginnings of recorded history to set forth their experiences of the powers that reside in nature. Through myths the inner domain of human consciousness is connected to the surrounding world. Shamans are selected for their knowledge of and special access to the world beyond the manifest. The great powers of this world, often perceived in the spirits of animals, are used for healing purposes. Artists sometimes experience the process of their creativity as occurring beyond themselves, tapping into a source in nature from which they draw that is shaped by their efforts but exists in another realm.

Small children also have quite ready access to this spirit world
— or have not yet had these experiences dismissed or reasoned away.
I recently met with a three-year-old girl who told me of her "real"
world, a world filled with animal and human figures commingled
in a complex melange of elements from the hylotropic and holotropic realms. For her the foxes and bears of the mythic domains
were as real as the day-to-day life with her parents and brother.
Yet she was in no way psychotic; she was able to navigate admira-
bly at school and at home and was considered by her teachers to
be a model child.

Disturbing emotions, such as great fear and sadness as well
as exaltation and joy, darkness as well as light, are associated with
the spiritual realm, which may account for some of our resistance
to opening ourselves to its reality. Psychoanalyst Hans Loewald
has described clearly the way we distance ourselves from the depths
of religious experience and the reason for this:

> Psychoanalysts tend to consider the idea of eternity, religious
> experiences connected with it, as well as the "timeless" expe-
> riences I described, in pragmatic fashion as useful and often
> necessary defenses, or as mental sanctuaries people must have
> to cope with the fear of death, castration, and with the trials,
> tribulations, and the transitoriness of human life. I do not
> doubt the truth of this view. But it is not the whole truth.
> I believe that "intimations of eternity" bring us in touch with
> levels of our being, forms of experiencing and of reality that
> themselves may be deeply disturbing, anxiety-provoking to
> the common-sense rationality of everyday life.[6]

Spiritual or religious experience calls forth the language of
the sacred, words like *soul, spirit, transcendence, reverence,* and
faith. Psychoanalysts and other dynamically oriented psychologists have tended to be uncomfortable with this language. Because
the sense of merger or fusion with the mother in early infancy,
recaptured in the therapeutic setting, has qualities much like the
sense of oneness of mystical experiences, we have sometimes made
the error of equating the two phenomena, reducing profound religious consciousness to infantilism or childish wish-fulfillment.
Freud himself denied the reality of the spiritual domain in his
own experience.[7] Recent writings on this subject have been much

more sophisticated and open to the significance of these matters.[8]

Many of us in the West, who have been educated in both our families and our schools in the epistemologies of rationalism and empiricism, have found ourselves cut off from the realms of the sacred, whereas virtually all other peoples throughout history have experienced its presence and central importance in their lives. According to historian of religions Mircea Eliade, "*All* history is in some measure a fall of the sacred, a limitation and diminution."[9] The separation of self from nature and the divine, of which nature is a supreme manifestation,[10] may be one of the great negative achievements of Western civilization, one which we are now desperately striving to undo before it is too late. How and why we have done this to ourselves are questions which take us beyond the reach of this paper. The answers lie in the extreme development of reason and empiricism — of which technology is a derivative — for the purpose of controlling and dominating one another and all of nature, at the expense of feeling and the intuitive ways of knowing that might have helped us live in greater harmony with other peoples and the natural world.

What, then, would *be* a spiritual point of view? It would include the following elements:

1. An attitude of appreciation, or a sense of awe, toward the mysterious in nature, including our own natures, and toward all of creation, resisting the tendency to explain the motives behind spiritual experience or belief. In Eliade's words, "There is always a kernel that remains refractory to explanation, and this indefinable, irreducible element perhaps reveals the real situation of man in the cosmos."[11] Joseph Campbell in his interviews with Bill Moyers spoke of the tendency to reduce mystery. "The mystery has been reduced to a set of concepts and ideas," he said, "and emphasizing these concepts and ideas can short-circuit the transcendent, connoted experience. An intense experience of mystery is what one has to regard as the ultimate religious experience."[12]

2. Opening ourselves to the experience of the cosmos and of all beings in nature as sacred. This has little to do with idealization or the denial of hostility or aggression. It is, rather, about reverence or respect, an openness to the possibility of value that

is hidden from our perception. In Christian theology this attitude, when applied to human beings, is sometimes called "exaltation" or a sense of the exalted nature of humankind.[13]

3. The application of a cosmological as contrasted with a materialist perspective on reality. This means thinking and experiencing systematically and opening ourselves to the possibility that there is a design and, if not harmony, at least appropriate relations in nature, including human relationships.

4. A subjective sense of hesitation or doubt, especially in the clinical setting, appreciating that this does not reflect unassertiveness or obsessionalism but facilitates a deepening of the therapeutic dialogue. In the words of Christian theologian Glen Tinder, "hesitation expresses a consciousness of the mystery of being and dignity of every person."[14]

5. A distrust of all human-made institutions, even as we will, of necessity, participate in them. This includes psychoanalytic institutes and departments of psychiatry and other professional organizations as well as political entities, such as nations, and even churches. For institutions may be essential in carrying out basic societal functions, but by requiring of us an identification with their purposes, rules, and reward systems, they may obstruct our relation to the numinous or holotropic and to spiritual experience itself. Institutions may stand as vehicles for expressions of congealed power on the part of individuals and groups, and will, perhaps inevitably, find the self-empowering experience of contact with the divine as threatening or subversive. For spiritual experience by its very nature ties us to the primary power in nature; elevates the confidence of individuals in their own thoughts, emotions, and perceptions; and diminishes blind loyalty to any humanly built structures. Established churches and other institutions may, paradoxically, be especially distrustful of spiritual experience and direct contact with the divine, since their power and reason for existing derive from their role as intermediaries setting the conditions of appropriate congregation and worship, while interpreting the nature of the divinity.

6. In the clinical setting a spiritual point of view means the development of an attitude toward emotionally troubled patients or clients that is less medical or pathology-focused while

stressing, nevertheless, the healing function of the therapeutic enterprise and the relief of suffering. The distinction here is subtle, a matter of emphasis. It means stressing our connection with our patients, rather than the differences, the shared fate and common source of our mutual pain and experience of what it is to be human. Personal growth and empowerment, even "enlightenment," would receive relatively greater emphasis than conflict resolution or cure.[15] As in the case of community psychiatry when it became a formal discipline in the 1960s, many of us will realize that we have been including a spiritual point of view in the practice of our discipline all along. We just have not called it that.

Increasing numbers of clinical practitioners, including psychoanalysts or psychoanalytically-oriented psychotherapists, and their clients are following what in religious traditions had been called a "spiritual path." Many are returning to the formal religions of their families, sometimes interpreting them in new ways, or joining other churches or religious groups, in order to discover or rediscover the spiritual core of the self from which they feel they have become disconnected. Others find the beginnings of a spiritual opening in psychoanalysis itself, sometimes modified by its practitioners, or in more traditional psychotherapies. The popularity of alternative forms of psychotherapy which emphasize spiritual techniques and opening is related to the spiritual hunger discussed at the beginning of this paper. The burgeoning in the West of meditation practice, largely derived from Eastern religions, and of spiritual retreats, also reflects the spiritual awakening and transformation that is occurring in our society. Buddhist theory and practice, with its emphasis on mindfulness and upon living in harmony with nature, has been particularly attractive to American clinicians, some of whom combine psychotherapy with Buddhist spiritual methods. Psychedelic substances, such as LSD and psilocybin mushrooms, which have the capacity to undo the culturally programmed obstacles to spiritual experience, though largely still illegal in the United States, have been important agents of spiritual opening and transformation for many psychotherapists. Increasing numbers of voices within the mainstream of American society are arguing that these agents should be made legal, at least for those conducting responsible research, in order to understand human behavior or neuropsychological functioning.[16]

A spiritual point of view requires that we modify or extend our notions of the self. *Self* is a bridging concept, joining psychology with sociology, philosophy, and religion. When used in a religious context, it is sometimes spelled with a capital S to suggest a vast, sacred, and ineffable domain. In recent years the ways that self is thought of in psychology and in religion have come closer together. Within psychoanalytic psychology self has connoted something which, though abstract, is fairly literal and bounded, a structure not very different from ego, the property of discrete individuals. The total self is an aggregate of more or less cohesive self-representations, both a locus and a source of agency. Self in a spiritual sense is something more mysterious or mythic, a space or possibility, a ground of being or source connected with the divine. Self in this sense is not discrete or limited to an individual, but a kind of fluid potential through which one connects with other selves and all of reality. There is even talk now of an "eco self" to indicate a flowing connection of a person with nature. The self in a spiritual sense is the locus of wounding and pain but also of transcendence and transformation.

Although *self* must remain an abstraction, we need to posit some such notion to account for the subjective sense that we exist. Through self we connect with others and with all of nature, and in this sense self is both a social or communal and a somewhat mystical concept. Buddhist poet and monk Thich Nhat Hanh speaks of "interbeing" to express this related or intersubjective aspect of self, while psychoanalyst George Klein uses the awkward but descriptive phrase "we go" to capture the social or connecting subjectivity of self.[17]

This connecting self is associated with desire, especially the desire to merge or fuse with another, or, as in the case of mystical experience, longing for oneness with all of creation or with God. There is a paradox for the self in this merger, for its fulfillment requires the death of the self or ego (in the psychological, small *s* sense), but from this death experiences of rebirth emerge. The cycles of ego death and rebirth, both terrifying and sublime, lie at the root of primary spiritual experience and have their first psychological analog in the phases of the birth process which are alternately largely blissful and secure (intrauterine life), terrifying and overwhelming (the crushing experience of passage through the birth canal), and sublime and transcendent (delivery and emergence into the world).[18]

Erik Erikson in some of his later writings has focused on the significance of the sense of *I* in religious or spiritual experience.[19] For Erikson the sense of *I* is a spiritual notion in that it derives from a core of personality that lies deeper or beyond psychosocial identity. It is the "place" (language fails us here) where Self connects beyond itself to something greater, with the divine or transcendent, and human beings discover their oneness with being itself. It is from the sense of *I* that existential issues derive: questions of life, death, and rebirth, or what Erikson calls the psychology of "ultimate concern."[20] According to Erikson, the *I* is at the "Center," "where the light is."[21] From the sense of *I* we derive our deepest values and intentions. It is the experiential core of identity behind the internalizations that create the sense of self in its purely psychosocial connotation. This deepest "place" of self is also associated with a sense of ultimate stability (perhaps because through the sense of *I* we are, ultimately, connected with the divinity), cohesiveness, and wholeness. Conversely, the absence of a core sense of *I* or self is associated with fragmentation and personality disruption. The tension between fragmentation and wholeness is a fundamental dilemma of contemporary life, at least in Western countries, and thus has important therapeutic implications.

The explicit inclusion of a spiritual point of view has significant implications for the practice of psychoanalysis and psychodynamic psychotherapy, although many of the elements that I would designate as belonging in this category are already becoming part of the way therapists function in the clinical setting. A spiritual view implies an attitude toward the patient or client as a person of special value. Inequalities of power are built into the therapeutic setting — accommodation, for example, to the therapist's schedule or differences of accessibility — but they need to be acknowledged as part of the clinical reality and not analyzed simply as elements of resistance or transference distortion. The enabling or empowering dimensions of the therapeutic relationship would receive relatively more emphasis in the healing process as compared to interpretation and insight. The transforming power of human connection, and of empathy and love, although always recognized as important in psychotherapy, would be more openly recognized and developed.[22]

A greater openness and sharing of one's own experiences, as appropriate, becomes a more accepted part of the therapeutic work, including admitting mistakes or apologizing for difficulties our own blindnesses or inadvertent actions may have caused or aggravated. The attitude of not knowing, of mystery and uncertainty discussed above, would be applied to the work with clients. Paradoxically this attitude is likely to bring forth greater awareness on the part of both client and therapist of hitherto unknown dimensions of self. In addition to elements in the unconscious warded off by specific defenses, this attitude of openness and not knowing can create a greater awareness of those culturally imbibed habits of thought — opinions, assumptions, and institutionally imposed ways of perceiving the world — that are unconscious by being so much a part of our daily lives (rather the way a fish might be unaware of the water it swims in) but restrict our ability to live and choose freely.

Wounds, loss, separation, grief, trauma, and emotional deprivations are the pathogenic forces of human life. Addressing the lasting impact of these forces and events that have occurred at various stages of a person's life is the bedrock of psychotherapeutic work from all of the psychoanalytic points of view. Once again, a spiritual point of view would bring a different emphasis. Established psychodynamic approaches tend to be concerned with the resolution of conflict, the repair of hurts and trauma, and the achievement of, or return to, a baseline of normal functioning. A spiritual point of view stresses — paradoxically again — the transformative power of the affects associated with biographical wounds and other disturbing historical experiences. The spiritual element derives from the belief, which lies at the boundary between experience and faith, that each person possesses within him- or herself a potential for wholeness. This does not mean, of course, that human beings do not have defects (especially biologically based ones), limitations, and irreparable wounds. It is, rather, a point of view which gradually establishes its validity through enabling greater wholeness. When therapy is conducted through a spiritual point of view the language of the sacred may creep into one's speech — words like *soul, divine, transcendent,* and *mystical* — as if no other way of speaking can quite capture the ineffable quality of this domain.

An emphasis on wholeness as a therapeutic objective carries with it the implication that some expression of social responsibility, or work for the larger human community, is part of a positive outcome. A commitment to the human future comes, inevitably, to be added to Freud's idea that a successful result in therapy is reflected in the ability to love and to work. This relates once again to our notion of self as connected with other selves, interrelated in an implicit web of ties that must, inevitably, expand our identifications beyond the boundaries of our families and ethnic groupings. The extraordinary success and healing power of AA and Twelve-Step work derives from this recognition of interconnectedness beyond the individual. The program of repair and community service that constitute the later steps of AA are directed at an expansion of spiritual growth. The twelfth step is introduced with, "Having had a spiritual awakening as a result of these steps, we tried to carry this message to alcoholics and to practice these principles in all our affairs."[23]

Another important dimension of the interconnectedness that lies at the heart of spiritual experience is the sense of continuity over time and the ties we feel to previous generations.[24] Native peoples place much more emphasis generally than we do in the West upon temporal continuity and planning for future generations. Psychiatrist Arthur Kornhaber has attributed the extraordinary strength of feeling between grandparents and grandchildren (and also great-grandparents and great-grandchildren) to the spiritual bond that connects us across generations. I have rarely seen such unmitigated joy as when my wife's mother at her eighty-fifth birthday party returned to the party after being called to the phone and announced with her arms thrown wide (a gesture none of us had seen her make for many years) and her eyes glistening, "I'm a great-grandmother."

Kornhaber tells the story of seven-year-old Annie, whom he had brought with several other elementary school children to visit a nursing home as part of an intergenerational program linking the two institutions. Annie went up to a seemingly lifeless old woman in a corner of the room, who, it turned out, had known her grandfather. In a few moments the woman was vitalized, transformed, "spirited." When Kornhaber asked Annie what she had done she replied, "Nothing at all, she just combed my hair." He concluded,

> This spiritual dimension of the self not only contains love, wonder, and joy but has the capacity to "illuminate" and "transform" the young and the old. Children seem to sense the spiritual qualities of older people and can transform what society generally sees as useless people into valuable elders. The child's view confers power and influence on the aged, who are often ignorant of their own influence. But when love is present, children are blind to the wrinkles that so often blind everyone else.[25]

Nonordinary or altered states of consciousness (largely unknown in the modern West, which has largely cut itself off from experience of the divine, but quite familiar to native peoples throughout the world) have extraordinary value in regaining spiritual power and recognition. These states can be achieved by methods which include hypnosis (abandoned by Freud with vast historical consequences for the therapeutic enterprise), meditation, mind-altering or "psychedelic" drugs used in the appropriate context, and psychoanalytically derived approaches which permit a suspension of linear consciousness and the emergence from the unconscious of elements of the holotropic or transpersonal realm.

Of particular value in this regard is the holotropic breathwork method developed by Stanislav and Christina Grof, which utilizes deep rapid breathing, evocative music, focal body work, and mandala drawing to gain access beyond the biographical level of experience to the perinatal period and the transpersonal realms, where feeling connection becomes possible with objects, creatures, and spirits that is not available to us in ordinary (hylotropic) states of consciousness. Thousands of therapists and their clients have found the Grof method to be a useful way to gain access to the healing power that lies in these deeper levels of the psyche. The holotropic breathwork method has a good deal in common with the traditional healing methods that shamans have used throughout the world, connecting their native "clients" with the transformative powers of animal spirits and other mythic forces that hold meaning in a particular culture. Perhaps the remarkable hold that our relationship with pets often has represents a vestige of the lost connection with the power of animal spirits in human life.

Most of the therapeutic methods that utilize nonordinary states of consciousness to access deeper realms of consciousness have in common an emphasis on the healing power of forces that are already present within the individual, a kind of inherent wisdom of the body/mind or soul. The therapist, healer, or spiritual healer in this context acts as a facilitator, a holder of the therapeutic ground, bringing forth what is already there but inaccessible to consciousness as the result of barriers erected by wounds or traumas from the past, or the restrictions of consciousness that are inherent in, or imposed by, Western society.

The threats on a global scale confronting us and much of the earth's life can be thought of as a spiritual crisis, for at its core it represents the separation of human beings from one another and of humankind from nature. The crisis is double-edged. On the one hand we must face massive destruction from wars in which technologically advanced weaponry, including nuclear devices, can cause death and suffering on a vast scale. At the same time we are experiencing a slower extinction of life through the erosion of the ecosystems that are themselves the life forms which support biologically more advanced organisms. What are the sources of these interrelated destructive processes, and how can we respond?

The global crisis derives from the techno-materialism of Western culture (and of those that imitate us in the search for power and a better life) which has now reached an extreme of destructiveness incompatible with the sustaining of life. The archetypal polarities of connection or closeness on the one hand and distancing and separation on the other are inherent dimensions of human nature. But the twin materialist quests for control of the earth's limited physical resources and for absolute security through the dominance of advanced weaponry have exaggerated these polarities to the extent that they have become a terminal threat to life.

Erik Erikson has called the extreme differentiation of one human group from another to the extent of denying the humanity of the other group "pseudospeciation."[26] Pseudospeciation reflects above all a kind of large group egotism, through which a people seeks to elevate its collective self-regard at the expense of another. Theologian Glen Tinder has described this process well.

Idealism in our time is commonly a form of collective pride. Human beings exalt themselves by exalting a group. Each one of course exalts the singular and separate self in some manner. In most people, however, personal pride needs reinforcement through a common ideal of emotion, such as nationalism. Hence the rise of collective pride. To exalt ourselves, we exalt a nation, a class, or even the whole of humanity in some particular manifestation like science. Such pride is alluring. It assumes grandiose and enthralling proportions yet it seems selfless, because not one person alone but a class or nation or some other collectivity is exalted. It can be at once more extreme and less offensive than personal pride.[27]

The polarizing and dichotomizing tendencies of the human mind become exaggerated in the context of hatred and fear. Ethnonational conflicts, with their complex histories of killing, loss, and grief, deepen these polarities in vicious cycles of destruction, rage, and distrust unless new leadership intervenes that can heal and transcend the conflicts. Traditional leaders are likely to accentuate the polarities by calls to just or holy wars in which the forces of good are perceived as attached exclusively to one's own cause and all negativity to the other's. The language of religion can be especially dangerous when placed in the service of these polarities, as it amplifies their emotional intensity by invoking the greater powers of the universe on behalf of the interests and conflicts of a particular group.

What is called for then is a means of discovering a wider human identity, not one that denies the polarities of nature and human feeling, but one that integrates them in a larger sense of purpose and connection. This shift would continue the process of spiritual transformation already taking place that is manifest now in the multitude of global initiatives that are striving to discover authentic international partnerships while respecting the uniqueness of ethno-national and cultural traditions. For individuals this process requires the discovery of a true core self of *I* through which we connect beyond ourselves to diverse *others*. This too is essentially a spiritual task. In Erikson's words, "Here an overweening conscience can find peace only by always believing that the budding 'I' harbors a truthfulness superior to that of all authorities because this truth is the covenant of the 'I' with God, the 'I' being more central and more persuasive than all parent images and moralities."[28] To achieve this evolution in practical terms will mean, at the least, a deliberate educational program aimed at teaching children, adolescents, and adults how to resist the threats, blandishments, and exhortations of traditional leaders who choose to play upon our polarizing tendencies, chiefly through manipulating the mass media, for the purpose of maintaining enmities and justifying the wars they create.

Lee Atwater when he was facing death found a "new spiritual presence" in his life:

> My illness helped me to see that what was missing in society is what was missing in me: a little heart, a lot of brotherhood. The '80s were about acquiring — acquiring wealth, power, prestige. I know. I acquired more wealth, power, and prestige than most. But you can acquire all you want and still feel empty. What power wouldn't I trade for a little more time with my family? What price wouldn't I pay for an evening with friends? It took a deadly illness to put me eye to eye with that truth, but it is a truth that the country, caught up in its ruthless ambitions and moral decay, can learn on my dime. I don't know who will lead us through the '90s, but they must be made to speak to this spiritual vacuum at the heart of American society, this tumor of the soul.[29]

Human beings grow when, in the confrontation with death, they are enabled to discover a new personal perspective, sacrificing their egoism before it is the body's time to die. This is what Eastern religions refer to as ego death. We are all, in literal terms, facing our own death. But what will be required of us, individually and collectively, for us to know the "spiritual vacuum" of our society? How can the transforming power of the confrontation with death on such a scale as we now confront on earth be experienced so that we may arrest the destruction we are creating for ourselves and much of our planet's life without having to reach, like Atwater, the point of no return? It seems to be a question worth asking, for the preservation of the planet is a fight worth fighting.

J. M. Coetzee in his novel about South African apartheid and its wounds, metaphorically titled *The Age of Iron* to describe an imperviousness to feeling and caring, gives these words to a dying white woman whose death is linked symbolically to the death of the culture:

> Such a good thing, life! Such a wonderful idea for God to have had! The best idea there had ever been. A gift, the most generous of all gifts, renewing itself endlessly through the generations.[30]

It is the responsibility of each of us to discover ourselves more fully, to become conscious of "Self," "Self-Conscious" in the larger sense that can ensure life will, indeed, be renewed through the generations.

NOTES

1. David Rapaport and Merton Gill, "The Points of View and Assumptions of Metapsychology," in *The Collected Papers of David Rapaport*, ed. Merton M. Gill (New York: Basic Books, 1977).

2. Heinz Kohut, *The Analysis of the Self*, Psychoanalytic Study of the Child, monograph no. 4 (New York: International Universities Press, 1971); Paul H. Ornstein, ed., *The Search for the Self: Selected Writings of Heinz Kohut 1950–1978* (New York: International Universities Press, 1978), vol. 1; Arnold Goldberg, ed., *Advances in Self Psychology* (New York: International Universities Press, 1980).

3. Philip Cushman, "Why the Self Is Empty," *American Psychologist* 45 (1990): 590–611.

4. Chana Ullman, *The Transformed Self: The Psychology of Religious Conversion* (New York: Plenum Press, 1989).

5. Barbara Marx Hubbard, *The Hunger of Eve* (Eastbound, Wash.: Island Pacific Northwest, 1989), pp. 179–80.

6. Hans W. Loewald, *Psychoanalysis and the History of the Individual* (New Haven and London, Conn.: Yale University Press, 1978), p. 69.

7. Sigmund Freud, "Civilization and Its Discontents," in *The Standard Edition of the Complete Psychological Works of Sigmund Freud*, ed. James Strachey (London: Hogarth Press, 1930), p. 65.

8. Ana-Maria Rizzuto, *The Birth of the Living God: A Psychoanalytic Study* (Chicago: University of Chicago Press, 1979); W. W. Meissner, *Psychoanalytic and Religious Experience* (New Haven, Conn.: Yale

University Press, 1984); Loewald, *Psychoanalysis*; Arthur Deikman, *The Observing Self: Mysticism and Psychiatry* (Boston: Beacon Press, 1982); Joseph H. Smith and Susan A. Handelman, eds., *Psychoanalysis and Religion* (Baltimore: Johns Hopkins University Press, 1990), vol. 2; K. Wilber, *Eye to Eye: The Quest for the New Paradigm* (Garden City, N.Y.: Anchor Books, 1983).

    9. Mircea Eliade, *Shamanism: Archaic Techniques of Ecstasy*, Bollingen Series 76 (Princeton, N.J.: Princeton University Press, 1974), p. 19.

    10. Thomas Berry, *The Dream of the Earth* (San Francisco: Sierra Club Books, 1990).

    11. Eliade, *Shamanism*, p. 14.

    12. Joseph Campbell (with Bill Moyers), *The Power of Myth* (New York: Doubleday, 1988), p. 209.

    13. Glen Tinder, "Can We Be Good Without God?" *Atlantic*, December 1989, p. 78.

    14. Ibid., p. 85.

    15. John E. Mack, "Changing Models of Psychotherapy: From Psychological Conflict to Human Empowerment," Center for Psychological Studies in the Nuclear Age, Cambridge, Mass., 1990; John E. Mack, "Toward a Psychology for Our Time," in *Psychology and Social Responsibility*, ed. Sylvia Staub and Paula Green (forthcoming).

    16. Winifred Gallagher, *American Health*, December 1990, pp. 60–67.

    17. George S. Klein, *Psychoanalytic Theory: An Exploration of Essentials* (New York: International Universities Press, 1976).

    18. Stanislav Grof, *Beyond the Brain* (New York: State University of New York Press, 1985).

    19. Erik H. Erikson, "The Galilean Sayings and the Sense of 'I,'" *Yale Review* (Spring 1981): 321–62; Hetty Zock, *A Psychology of Ultimate Concern* (Amsterdam: Rodopi, 1990).

    20. Zock, *A Psychology*.

    21. Erikson, "Galilean Sayings."

    22. Alfred Margulies, *The Empathetic Imagination* (New York: W. W. Norton & Co., 1989).

    23. *Alcoholics Anonymous: Twelve Steps and Twelve Traditions* (New York: Alcoholics Anonymous World Services, 1977), p. 109.

    24. Arthur Kornhaber, *Between Parents and Grandparents* (New York: St. Martin's Press, 1986).

    25. Arthur Kornhaber, *Vital Connections: The Grandparenting Newsletter*, (Fall 1990), p. 2.

26. Erik H. Erikson, *Gandhi's Truth* (New York: W. W. Norton & Co., 1969).

27. Tinder, "Can We Be Good?" p. 78.

28. Erikson, *Gandhi's Truth*, pp. 117–18.

29. Lee Atwater and T. Brewster, "Lee Atwater's Last Campaign," *Life*, February 1991, p. 67.

30. J. M. Coetzee, *The Age of Iron* (New York: Random House, 1990), p. 109.

The Liberal Discourse on Violence
BHIKHU PAREKH

I INTEND TO EXAMINE the way in which violence is generally conceptualized and debated in such liberal democracies as Britain, France, and the United States. My concern, therefore, is not with the formal liberal philosophical discourse on violence as developed by a long line of thinkers from Thomas Hobbes to John Rawls, but rather with the practical liberal political discourse on violence as it actually occurs in mature liberal democracies. I shall argue that although this liberal discourse takes different forms in different countries depending on their history and culture, it is embedded in and profoundly shaped by a shared body of assumptions about humankind and society and displays common structural features.

I

The political systems in Britain, France, West Germany, Canada, the United States, and other Western countries are regularly referred to as "liberal democracies." While this is a true characterization at one level, it is inadequate at another. Most of us would agree that a political system is liberal if it establishes the rule of law, civil and political liberties, constitutionally guaranteed basic rights, and a limited government based on internal checks and balances. And we would agree that it is democratic if the government is elected by and accountable to the electorate constituted on the basis of universal franchise and is responsive to public opinion and pressure. Western political systems satisfy these conditions and are rightly called liberal democracies. However, it is not difficult to imagine political systems which might satisfy them but which we would hesitate to call liberal democracies. Take a political system in which elections to the national legislature are not direct but indirect, in which different ethnic or religious communities form separate electorates and are subject to different systems of law, or in which the national legislature is based on a system of corporate representation.[1] Although such a system is both liberal and democratic in the sense outlined earlier, it is radically different from its Western counterpart.[2]

The difference lies in the fact that Western liberal democracies take the *individual* as the ultimate unit of political life and organize their liberal and democratic institutions around individuals. The individual possesses and exercises the right to vote and enjoys civil and political liberties as an individual, not as a member of a specific group. In other words, political systems can be liberal-democratic in several different ways, the Western being but one of them. The Western liberal democracy is an association of individuals, not a federation of groups or a community of communities. It allows, even encourages, communities, but they have no legal and political status, are not bearers of rights and obligations, and do not constitutionally mediate between the individual and the state.

A new and naturalistic definition of the individual gained currency in Europe from the seventeenth century onwards and gave rise to the individualistic conception of humankind and society.[3] It inspired the struggle for liberty in moral, political, economic, and social areas of life, culminating in the nineteenth century in what we have come to call liberal democracies, in which the terms *individualism* and *liberalism* became interchangeable.

According to this view, first intimated by the medieval nominalists and fully articulated by Hobbes, humans are an individual substance of a rational nature, as Boethius had put it in an influential definition.[4] The reference to "individual substance" is striking and represents a significant departure from the earlier views of Augustine and Saint Thomas, not to mention those of Plato and Aristotle. In the individualist view the human being is a natural and self-contained unit unambiguously marked off from the rest of the world. The body is not an appendage, but a criterion of reality and the necessary basis of one's self-consciousness and identity. The body, signifying both matter and particularity, thus acquires ontological significance and dignity which it had rarely enjoyed before.

In the individualist view the individual is endowed with such interrelated powers and capacities as reason, will, and self-consciousness which make for a self-determining and self-directing being. One is capable of abstracting and distinguishing oneself from one's environment, confronting it as an independent being, weighing alternative courses of action, and choosing, willing, and acting on one of them. As a self-determining being the individual is above all an agent, an initiator of actions, a being capable of interrupting an ongoing event and starting a new chain of events. It is because one is capable of self-determination that one is a moral person and has dignity. Since the capacities that make for a person are intrinsic to the human species, their absence in some people is a regrettable deviation from the norm. Though idiots, lunatics, and severely mentally handicapped men and women might be little different from animals and sometimes even worse, they too therefore have dignity and ought not to be treated on a par with animals and inanimate objects.

As a self-determining agent or person, an individual is responsible for the consequences of his or her actions. As long as one is not physically overpowered, hypnotized, or otherwise deprived of one's powers of choice and will, the individual is deemed to be autonomous and accountable for his or her actions. One is not entitled to say that he was starving and had no alternative but to steal a loaf of bread in order to stay alive; that her mother was dying of cold and she had to steal a blanket she eventually intended to return; that his personality had remained undeveloped because of his poor background and upbringing; or that her capacities of choice and will were gravely debilitated as a result of having been deserted by her parents and brought up by an ill-managed institution. Since the individual is abstracted from social background and circumstances, these backgrounds and circumstances are not co-agents of his or her actions. The individual stands alone, facing the world in sovereign isolation and exercising unconditioned freedom of choice and will. He who blames his upbringing and social circumstances implicitly concedes that he is not a full human being and forfeits his claim to dignity, respect, independence, and equality. She cannot demand the rights accruing to a person and disown the concomitant responsibility for her actions.

In the liberal view an individual's responsibility for his or her actions is reduced or eliminated only when the powers of choice and will are diminished or obliterated. For obvious reasons idiots and lunatics are not responsible for their actions. An agent who lacks them at the time of action, as in the case of temporary amnesia or loss of consciousness, has only a limited responsibility or none at all for her actions. If she is in full possession of them at the time of her action, she can still claim diminished responsibility or total exemption from it if she can show that her choice and will were not hers but someone else's. When a mugger asks me to surrender my wallet, to steal someone's car, or to hit an innocent passer-by on pain of severe physical harm, my action is not mine. It is not a product of my choice but his; I am simply an instrument of his will; I follow not my aim but his. At one level the choice *was* mine, for I could have refused to comply with his demand and risked the consequences. In the individualist tradition people are presumed to be beings who wish to, and have a right to, guard themselves against physical harm. A choice made against the background of physical harm is therefore not regarded as a choice at all.

An apparently similar constraint might be placed on me by my circumstances. Faced with the threat of starvation or the prospect of my mother's death, I might have no alternative but to steal your wallet. For the individualist my action is qualitatively different from one in which I steal at a mugger's behest. The mugger wills my action for me; that is, he requires me to do a specific thing. By contrast, though my circumstances confront me with distressing alternatives and put me under severe pressure, they do not compel or require me to do a specific thing. I could have anticipated my predicament and made adequate provision for it, or I could have explained my situation to a friend or a neighbor and asked for help. My circumstances do not compel me to steal, overwhelm my will, and paralyze my powers of choice; nor do they have the urgency and immediacy characteristic of my encounter with the mugger. Since my powers of choice and will are formally unimpaired, I remain responsible for the theft.[5]

As a self-determining agent the individual in the liberal view is responsible for those consequences of her actions that she intended or could have reasonably foreseen; that is, those that would not have occurred without, and are thus directly traceable to, her actions. Her moral responsibility is coextensive with her causal responsibility, and causality is defined in positive and active terms. If I push a drunkard into a puddle and he dies, I am responsible for his death because I intended and willed it and initiated a chain of events culminating in it. If he fell into it by accident or was pushed into it by someone else, I bear no causal and moral responsibility for his death. If I could have saved his life but did not, I bear no or only a minimum responsibility for his death. Causality is taken to imply agency, initiation, active engagement, which is absent in my case. The fact that I could have interrupted the chain of events, and that my failure to do so was as much a cause of his death as someone's initial act of pushing him, does not find much favor in individualist jurisprudence. In some Western liberal democracies, but not in Britain, I could be punished for not saving his life if I could have done so without much hardship. However, the punishment is extremely mild and imposed under what is suggestively called a "Good Samaritan law," implying that saving a dying person is an act of charity, not a matter of moral obligation.

In the individualist view the state is held together by common allegiance to a public authority based on people's consent. Their membership in it confers on them a common identity as citizens. Citizens enter into all manner of relationships with one another and form countless groups and associations. There is no overarching entity encompassing these groups other than the state. What is called *society* is only a misleading way of describing the totality of relationships subsisting between individuals. As Mrs. Thatcher has repeatedly remarked, "There is no such thing as society."

Since society is a fiction, no one can be a "member" of it. She can be a member of the state, which is what we mean by citizenship, but there is no corresponding membership of society. A society is not a moral agent and cannot be a subject of moral judgment. It cannot be a cause of, and held responsible for, the circumstances in which its "members" might find themselves. To blame society, or the so-called social structure, for their misfortunes is to talk nonsense, as Hayek, Nozick, and others have argued. Since society is a fiction, individuals can have no obligations to it. All moral obligations are to other individuals or to the state.[6]

For the liberal, the state stands between order and disorder, between civilized life and anarchy. Its primary concern is to protect self-determining individuals in the exercise of their autonomy, and to enable them to make their own uncoerced choices. It can do so only by acquiring a monopoly on the right to use force. All other uses of force are forbidden except under clearly specified conditions. The state ensures the autonomy of its citizens by creating a framework of rights and protecting them in their exercise and enjoyment of them. To be a citizen is to be a bearer of rights and obligations, including the right to activate the coercive machinery of the state when one's rights are threatened.

However, while the state's monopoly of force is needed to protect its citizens against each other's interferences, it can itself become a threat. Its exercise of force is therefore strictly regulated in such interconnected ways as the rule of law, justifiable rights against the state, a free press, universal suffrage, free elections, civil and political liberties, and a system of checks and balances built into the structure of government. Though force is the *ultima ratio* of the state and constitutes the final sanction behind the law, the state is regarded as a qualitatively different institution from muggers, thieves, and robbers who also rely on force to get their way. The state's use of force is governed by publicly stated rules and procedures and exercised with clinical precision and impartiality. It acts through laws, which lay down in general terms what classes of actions are permitted or forbidden and what penalties attach to the latter. They are rules, not commands. They exert pressure, but they do not coerce or compel. They direct but do not dictate actions. Citizens therefore remain free to choose and pursue their own goals within the framework of the law. Unlike subjection to the will of another individual which spells loss of freedom, as in the case of slaves, serfs, and servants, subjection to impersonal laws is the very basis of freedom.

II

The liberal democratic discourse on violence is embedded in the moral and political theory whose barest outlines were sketched above.[7] Since the state enjoys a monopoly on force and private individuals may use it only under rare circumstances specified by the law, the distinction between legitimate and illegitimate force is crucial in a liberal democracy. The distinction is often expressed as that between force and violence. Force is authorized; violence is an unauthorized use of force.

Unlike the state's use of force, which is announced in advance and regulated by rules and procedures, the unauthorized private use of force is unregulated, unpredictable in its origin, and indiscriminate in its targets. As such, in the liberal discourse violence is invariably associated with passion, rage, anger, and suddenness. It "flares up," "erupts," "spreads like wildfire," "breaks out," and is in the nature of an "outburst." It is noisy, dramatic, visible, involves guns and knives, and has clearly identifiable agents and victims. Not surprisingly the terrorist, the murderer, the hijacker, the rapist, and the mugger become the paradigms of violence.

In the liberal discourse violence is associated with harm to the body and, to a lesser extent, to property. Since in liberalism the body is defined in naturalistic terms, the body acquires unprecedented ontological, epistemological, moral, and political significance. Violence is therefore defined in physical terms so that the infliction of physical harm is violence, but that of psychic or moral harm is not. Physical suffering, more than any other type of suffering, dominates the liberal moral imagination.

It is because so much importance is attached to physical harm that the threat of it is taken to reduce or even eliminate the agent's responsibility for her action. When I comply with a mugger's wish, my action is not mine but his because I had no "real" choice in the matter. Similarly a woman consenting to sexual intercourse under threat of physical harm is considered to be raped and has a legal redress; one doing so because otherwise she would not get the job she desperately needs to avoid starvation, or would be failed in her examinations, is not. The liberal preoccupation with physical harm is evident also in almost all the traditional descriptions of the state of nature. Apparently men and women fear physical harm or violent death far more than anything else.

In the liberal discourse, violence is confined to deliberate human acts. A mugger is guilty of violence; an employer who gives me the choice of facing starvation or accepting barest subsistence wages is not. The law forbids a person to cause me physical harm; it did not for years, and in some cases it does not even today, punish an employer for making employees work under conditions in which they are certain to catch serious diseases, develop bodily disorders, and even meet a premature and painful death. Reasons for the distinction are the ones mentioned earlier. The mugger leaves me no choice, denies my dignity as a self-determining being, and compels me to act in a specific manner. My relation to him is involuntary in the sense that I neither sought him out nor complied with his demand out of my own volition. By contrast I am free to reject the employer's offer and am a willing party to whatever arrangement we might make.

Since liberals understand causality in positive and active terms, they consider an individual guilty of violence only if she intended or could have reasonably foreseen the physical harm she caused to another. A woman who stabs me, and a terrorist who plants a bomb, are both guilty of violence, whereas a man who fails to save an old woman from a mugger's fatal attack, or a child from drowning, even when he could have done so without any harm to himself, is not. In the liberal moral theory a qualitative distinction is drawn between positive and negative action. In the former the outcome is willed; in the latter it is simply allowed to happen. Morally, therefore, killing a woman and letting her die are considered qualitatively different acts, the former being murder, the latter a case of neglect entailing no or minimum legal punishment. Since an action is judged on the basis of whether or not it violates the law, its goals or purposes do not form part of the judgment. In liberal democratic jurisprudence, no distinction is drawn between criminal and political violence. All violence is equally criminal, irrespective of the agent's intentions and objectives.

III

I now wish to outline those states of affairs that the liberal discourse on violence distorts, obscures, suppresses, or marginalizes, and then explore what theoretical devices enable it to do so.

In the United States African-Americans live, on average, about six years less than whites.[8] This means that nearly twenty-five million people die six years before the rest. Since all the available evidence indicates that the state of health and longevity improve with the betterment of economic circumstances, most of these deaths are premature and avoidable. The difference in Britain between the life spans of the unskilled and the professional classes is around five years. This means that nearly a million and a half people die five years earlier than their better-off fellow citizens.

Again, British prisons are grossly overcrowded and provide another example of a state of affairs obscured by liberal individualism. Prisoners are locked up in bleak cells, sometimes two and even three in a room not large enough for even one. They defecate in buckets provided in their rooms and empty them each morning. They are insulted, degraded, treated with contempt, and sometimes beaten up by other prisoners and even officers. Some commit suicide; many more contract avoidable diseases. Violence smolders just below the surface and expresses itself in countless small acts of harm and injury not brutal enough to meet its official definition. Such prisons hardly represent a restrictive use of force. In fact, force is exercised in the spirit of violence and brutalizes both its agents and its victims.

One could list similar cases of physical suffering and harm in other Western liberal democracies. At a different level, one could also point to millions in the Third World whose lives would have been spared and whose heartbreaking suffering avoided with a little more imagination, generosity, and concerted action on the part of the Western states and their affluent citizens.

By any definition of the term, including the liberal, the cases of physical suffering, distress, and premature and painful deaths described above constitute violence. They involve physical harm and injury to human beings; unlike floods, earthquakes, and other natural calamities, they are human in origin; their existence and incidence are not unknown to us; and they can be either prevented or alleviated by human efforts. It is striking that in the liberal democratic discourse they are not called violence.

This raises two questions: Why do liberal democracies concentrate most of their attention on some forms of violence and not on the ones we have described, even when no significant difference seems to separate the two? And why do their morally sensitive citizens feel troubled by the criminal violence as represented by muggers, murderers, terrorists, and rapists but remain indifferent to the far more extensive violence going on behind their backs and to which they are themselves sometimes a party? The explanation lies in the unarticulated and unquestioned assumptions at the heart of political individualism.

First, since violence in a liberal democracy is generally understood as unauthorized force, there is a systematic tendency to confuse *violent acts* with *acts of violence.* In a liberal democracy, therefore, the terrorists, muggers, and murderers become the paradigms of violence, with the result that the silent, noiseless, systematic, and routinized violence either is not called violence or is allowed to fall out of view. Physical harm can be caused in a variety of ways, the use of physical force being only one of them. A man who poisons or starves his child to death is guilty of violence as much as one who shoots her. Not all acts of violence are, or need be, done in a violent manner.[9]

Once we realize this, a number of phenomena we otherwise overlook become visible. We stop concentrating on the terrorists and murderers, and begin to look closely at the drug companies which try out lethal drugs and devices on poor people in our own societies and especially in the Third World; at the multinational companies whose low wages, substandard working conditions, and dangerous technology cause acute physical suffering and harm in the poorer parts of the world; and at the airlines and shipping companies who take risks with their passengers and employees. We stop believing that only the unauthorized use of force leads to violence, and start taking a critical look at the government. We examine its domestic and foreign policies to see if they risk their citizens' health under pressures from vested interests, license unfit vehicles, allow people to drink and drive and slaughter thousands on our roads, lock up and impose unduly heavy sentences on a disproportionately large number of people from specific ethnic groups, destabilize foreign governments, provoke unnecessary wars between new and immature countries, engage in clandestine terrorism, and allow inmates to live in inhumane conditions in prisons. So long as we concentrate on violent acts, our eyes remain turned to the frightening deeds going on in the darkness of the night at the margins of our society. Once we appreciate that acts of violence can be performed nonviolently we begin to notice the structured, routinized, and invisible violence going on right at the heart of our societies, in broad daylight, in our name, and allegedly in our interest.

Second, the agency-oriented moral theory underlying liberal democracy blocks large areas of physical harm from our view. In the individualist view the agent is uniquely responsible for the consequences of her actions. When confronted with situations of physical harm, say the deaths of impoverished elderly people from hypothermia during a bitter winter, the only appropriate question is who is responsible for them. Since none of us caused them, none of us is responsible. And since none of us is responsible for them, none of us has a duty to stop causing them. The deaths do not fall within the moral jurisdiction of any of us. In an agency-oriented approach physical harm is morally relevant only as a consequence of someone's deliberate action.

The limitations of this approach are obvious. It renders the elderly people's deaths morally invisible and unimportant. Since they are not *a consequence* of our deliberate actions, they need not be *of any consequence* to us. On the basis of our liberal individualism, we need not feel guilty about them. The individualist approach defines causality in extremely narrow terms and ignores the fact that — insofar as I could have prevented the elderly people's deaths — I remain partly responsible for them. Furthermore, the individualist approach equates duty with responsibility. I do have a duty to relieve the suffering caused by my actions. However, my duties go beyond my responsibility. Suffering has a moral claim on me, and I have a duty to alleviate it even if I am not causally responsible for it.

Third, the narrow individualist notion of causality conceals our moral responsibility for a wide range of harm. When causality is defined in positive and active terms, the whole area of negative action escapes our view. For example, A, who pushed a drunkard into a puddle, is causally and morally responsible for his death. But B, a passer-by who saw him drown and did nothing to save him, is not. This view of causality is obviously untenable. The drunkard died because he drowned in a puddle. He drowned because A pushed him into it, and also because B refused to pull him out. B's refusal to do so or call for help was as much a deliberate act as A's. She knew, or could be reasonably expected to know, the consequences of her action. In willing the action, she willed its consequences. It is true that A initiated a chain of events. However, by doing nothing to interrupt it, B willed its continuation and is an accomplice to A's deed. A was motivated by ill will, B by callous indifference to human suffering. Though the two acts and their motives are morally different, the difference is not so great as wholly to exonerate B.[10]

Fourth, the individualist approach concentrates on *acts* and ignores *situations* of violence. When a prisoner commits suicide, we treat it as a case of self-inflicted violence. The facts of the matter are far more complex. The prisoner committed suicide in an institution in which he or she lived in a specific way, was related to other prisoners and prison officers in a certain manner, and was constantly exposed to a particular kind of climate. Our prisons are suffused with the spirit of violence, vengeance, anger, and contempt. The prisoner's self-inflicted violence was not an isolated act nor wholly voluntary; it was an integral part of and largely caused by the way of life obtaining in a prison. At a different level, the same was true of factory workers in nineteenth-century Britain. To be a worker was to work under physically debilitating conditions, to earn meager wages, to be exposed to daily humiliations and early death. No one killed the workers; they were placed in a situation in which early death and physical suffering were inescapable.

Fifth, in the individualist moral theory there is a constant tendency to concentrate on motives. It is assumed that an agent's actions reflect the agent's character; that if there is violence in those actions there must be violence in the agent; that all violence is a product of ill will, malice, or malevolence. This view is untenable. It is, of course, true that a man who hates another person is more likely to harm him or her than if he does *not* hate that person. It does not, however, follow that only those ill-disposed to others do violence to them. Eichmann did not hate Jews; he only did his duty as he saw it. Stalin did not bear ill will to kulaks; he was only interested in industrializing the Soviet Union, and since that involved killing a few thousand kulaks, he did not mind the "price." The passer-by in our example was not ill-disposed to the drunkard; she was simply callous. Judging an act is quite a different activity from judging its agent. It involves different considerations, has different logical structures, and serves different purposes. Unlike the motive, an act is an objective and worldly event, part of a complex set of ongoing events and enjoying a life and identity of its own. So long as an agent could have reasonably foreseen its consequences, she is responsible for them, whatever her motive.

So long as we think in terms of motives, we lack the conceptual tools to adequately characterize and evaluate such actions. Once we get away from motives and concentrate on what I have called dispositions, a different judgment becomes possible. The man who pushed the drunkard might have done so in anger, been after his money, or had a score to settle or a dislike for drunkards. By contrast, the passer-by might have been guided by no such considerations, and might simply be callous, unconcerned, and lacking in that elementary concern for another human being which distinguishes a moral from an amoral being. It is at least arguable that the latter's conduct is morally more reprehensible.

Sixth, the rigid distinction drawn in the individualist approach between subjection to the will of another individual and to the law blinds the liberal to the variety of ways in which the state might become a party to, and even a patron of, a vast system of violence. A liberal democracy ensures the autonomy of its citizens by establishing a relatively inviolable system of rights. Although this is not often appreciated, rights involve force and violence in at least three important ways. First, they help define violence in the sense of indicating what constitutes my life, liberty, and property, and what amounts to an interference with or violation of them. Second, they are ultimately guaranteed and enforced by the coercive power of the state, which even in a liberal democracy is sometimes little distinguishable from violence. The nineteenth-century British state which hanged hundreds for all manner of petty crimes against person and property could hardly be said to have used its monopoly of force merely for restrictive or protective purposes. Third, rights justify the state's use of force and even violence. In a liberal democracy, to say that the state used force and even violence on its citizens in order to safeguard and enforce the rights of others is to provide one of the most powerful and least contentious justifications of it. In setting up a system of rights the state thus necessarily sets up a system of violence; it lays down what kind of violence its citizens may not do to one another and what kind and quantity of force it will use against them if they do. One person's right is another person's coercion. Rights involve both benefits and burdens, the opportunity to use the coercive power of the state to one's advantage *and* against others. In a liberal democracy we tend to concentrate on rights and ignore their ugly underside.

The state does not establish rights in a vacuum. They are embedded in an ongoing structure of social relationships in which people occupy specific positions, are related to one another in specific ways, and enjoy or suffer moral, cultural, psychological, and other advantages or disadvantages derived from their social positions. The right to property guarantees protection to those who already have property. As for the rest, it only promises protection if they are lucky enough to acquire it in future. Though the right is formally available to all, in effect it is exercised and enjoyed by a few. In protecting rights the state undertakes to protect all that is substantively gained by exercising them. Since the gains are unequal, the state's services are unequally available to its citizens. Though formally impartial, in practice its use of force is selective and partial, and bears disproportionately heavily on the disadvantaged by the prevailing pattern of distribution of rights. Unlike their better-off fellow citizens, they experience the state as a punitive rather than a protective institution.

Since rights in an unequal society have unequal consequences, in creating a system of rights the state creates conditions necessary for the emergence and perpetuation of economic and other inequalities. Since these inequalities result in shorter life spans, physical suffering and harm, vulnerability to diseases, empty and deeply scarred lives, and such other consequences discussed earlier, the state cannot escape at least part of the responsibility for them. If it had established a different system of rights, these consequences would not have followed. Though it did not itself cause the violence, it created conditions it fully knew would result in it.

Finally, the individualist view underlying the liberal democracy finds it exceedingly difficult to accommodate the notion of shared responsibility indispensable to organized life. An isolated individual initiating a chain of events and accepting full responsibility for the consequences of her actions has little relevance to political life where we act as members of a collectivity and are responsible for what it does in our name and our interest. The responsibility is greater in a liberal democracy than under most other political systems. The government here is elected by us, derives its authority from us, can be swayed by public pressure, speaks and acts in our name, and claims to pursue our collective interests.

Above all, it explicitly invokes the authority of public opinion to justify its actions, and claims to follow specific policies because the "public" wants them. Members of Parliament and ministers use their daily mail and expressions of public protest as determinant of the range of options available to them.

In one way or another we are thus morally implicated in the deeds of our government. Because our rights and liberties are greater in a liberal democracy, so are our responsibilities. To be a citizen is to incur an obligation to keep a critical eye on the government lest it should act in our name in a manner we disapprove of, and to use all available channels of legitimate pressure to restrain it from doing so. Its actions *are* our collective actions, for the consequences of which we are collectively responsible. That the shared responsibility cannot be divided up and apportioned to each of us individually does not absolve us of our joint responsibility. The individualist view which makes an individual responsible for the consequences of his actions does not take account of this. Indeed it cannot. It can deal only with actions *uniquely* initiated by the agent and whose consequences can be directly traced to her, which is not at all the case in politics. The individualist view is largely applicable to personal life; when extended to collective — especially political — life, it has the paradoxical consequence of obscuring an agent's moral responsibility for even the most horrendous consequences to which he is a party.

IV

I outlined above some of the reasons why the liberal discourse on violence is selective and biased, and explored some of the ways in which it obscures, marginalizes, or defines out of existence several disturbing forms of violence and our responsibility for them. If we are to uncover and confront the full extent of violence and human suffering in our society and in the world at large, we need to reconsider and revise many of the individualist assumptions underlying the theory and practice of liberal democracy. In particular, we need to develop more satisfactory conceptions of the individual, agency, causality, duty, negative action, and collective responsibility. It would help greatly if we were to reverse the individualist schema and place the victim rather than the agent at the center of our inquiry. Rather than ask *if* and *how* we are causally and morally responsible for physical harm to others, we should ask *why* millions suffer distress, injury, pain, and premature deaths, and what we could do to prevent and alleviate them. We would still need to raise the question of causal and moral responsibility, but it would largely have an instrumental significance and be located in a context that does not even for a moment distract our gaze from the reality of human suffering.

NOTES

1. Unable to bring their civil law under a common legal system, the Indian government in 1988 floated the idea of a separate legal system for Muslims, giving the Muslim woman a right to decide at the time of marriage by what system of laws she wished to be governed. Mercifully the proposal did not find much favor.

2. It was one of the recurrent complaints against the British political system in the 1960s and early 1970s that it was increasingly turning Britain into a corporate state. Since corporatism is invariably associated with fascism, the complaint evoked a good deal of sympathy.

3. For a fuller discussion see Bhikhu Parekh, *Marx's Theory of Ideology* (Oxford: Croom Helm, 1982), pp. 36ff.

4. Boethius's definition of *persona* was widely accepted by medieval thinkers.

5. This contrast is a recurrent theme in almost all liberal writers. In recent years it has been emphasized by Isaiah Berlin, *Four Essays on Liberty* (Oxford: Oxford University Press, 1969); Michael Oakeshott, *On Human Conduct* (Oxford: Clarendon Press, 1975); F. A. Hayek, *The Constitution of Liberty* (London: Routledge & Kegan Paul, 1960); and Robert Nozick, *Anarchy, State and Utopia* (London: Basic Books, 1974).

6. Both Hayek and Oakeshott forcefully make the point in the works cited above.

7. I am primarily concerned to discuss not liberal thinkers but the actual practice of liberal democracies. What follows is derived from newspapers, political periodicals, parliamentary speeches, and radio and televison discussions in Britain, the United States, and other Western nations.

8. For a good discussion see Ted Honderich, *Violence for Equality* (Harmondsworth: Penguin, 1976), pp. 16ff; and Peter Singer, *Prac-

tical Ethics (Cambridge: Cambridge University Press, 1979), pp. 158ff.

9. For a good discussion see John Harris, "The Marxist Conception of Violence," *Philosophy and Public Affairs* 4 (1974).

10. Honderich makes a powerful case against the dominant distinction between positive and negative action in his *Violence for Equality*, pp. 58ff. See also Harris, "The Marxist Conception of Violence," pp. 202ff.

Author Index

Subject Index